FIVE GO TO WAR

The Glorious Five Nations Story

Richard Cockerill
shows how much it
means to wear
the England jersey

FIVE GO TO WAR
The Glorious Five Nations Story

MAIN TEXT BY MIKE WOOD

generation
PUBLICATIONS

Main text by Mike Wood

Designed by Adrian Waddington and Rob Kelland

Sub-edited by Mike Richards

Edited by Phil McNeill

Published by David Crowe and Mark Peacock

With thanks to:
Eve Cossins, Mark Crossland, Lyn Evans, Pauline Evans, Ailsa Jensen, Catherine McNeill,
Deanne Pearson, John Scott, Paul Sudbury, John Vaughan, Ken Vaughan, Caroline Warde,
Neil Loft and Justin Davies at Allsport and Heather Quest at Rhino Rugby Ltd,
and to Hayters for the statistics

Special thanks to:
Bill Beaumont, Richard Cockerill, Ieuan Evans, Gavin Hastings,
Willie John McBride, Jean-Pierre Rives, Pierre Villepreux and Keith Wood

First published in Great Britain in 1999 by Generation Publications
11-12 Tottenham Mews, London W1P 9PJ
generationgroup@btconnect.com

Text copyright © Generation Publications 1999

A catalogue record for this title is available from the British Library

ISBN 1 903009 11 1

Production by Mike Powell & Associates (01494 676891)
Origination by Colour Systems Ltd, London
Printed and bound in Italy by Giunti Industrie Grafiche

PHOTOGRAPHIC ACKNOWLEDGEMENTS
All photographs by Allsport and the Hulton Getty Collection, except Rhino Rugby, page 10

Contents

Wonderful Memories

BY
WILLIE JOHN
McBRIDE

Willie John McBride wrote his name in rugby history when, as captain of the British Isles, he led the first visiting team to win a series in South Africa. But he also played a small matter of 53 Five Nations matches for Ireland between 1962 and 1975 – and the memories linger on...

Time changes everything and in some ways it is sad to see the end of the Five Nations Championship. However, I welcome Italy into the most important rugby championship in the northern hemisphere and believe that it will add flavour to the entire tournament.

I had the privilege of playing in the Five Nations from 1962-75 and naturally I have some wonderful memories. My first game was at Twickenham in 1962 and what a frightening experience to run on to the ground at so-called HQ to a reception from the largest crowd I had ever played before up to that date. We were 'stuffed' – but there were better days when we won at Twickers. Why is it that we all love to win at Twickenham?

Then of course there was the French experience and it didn't matter whether it was in Dublin or Paris, the atmosphere was special. How the French supporters enjoyed themselves – I could never understand how they smuggled those French cockerels into Dublin, and indeed into the ground at Lansdowne Road.

I will never forget my first game against France, in Dublin. When a scrum turned into a mêlée, there was a chorus of verbal abuse from the French forwards, which we did not understand, but it did the trick for us – we had obviously upset them and we won.

Princes Street in Edinburgh was also an experience on match weekend and all those men in skirts – many a battle won and lost at Murrayfield, it's a pity the terracing is gone.

Cardiff Arms Park was another story. I didn't experience many wins there. I hate to say this, but Wales were on a different level from the rest of us in the Seventies. What a privilege to play against the likes of Gareth Edwards, Barry John, Phil Bennett, JPR Williams, Gerald Davies and many more superb Welsh players over those years. I also treasure the privilege of being on the same pitch with most of them for the Lions, especially in 1971 and 1974.

But it was Dublin and Lansdowne Road that stood out for me – many a good win and many a good night was had. I recall beating Wales 14-0 and coming off the pitch when a rather enthusiastic Irishman threw his arms around me and said: "And they were bloody lucky to get nil."

I never had the good fortune to be on a team which won the Triple Crown, but I did play on some great Irish teams who performed with passion. However, a special year for me was 1974 when Ireland won the championship and I was captain.

I'm sure all the players who have taken part in the Five Nations Championship will have their own memories, and I look forward to reading what Bill Beaumont, Ieuan Evans, Gavin Hastings, Jean-Pierre Rives, Pierre Villepreux, Keith Wood and Richard Cockerill have to say in these pages.

The game was about people and personalities in my day – now it is professional with a different emphasis. Change is never wrong, provided it is for the better, and I trust that the Six Nations will provide its own personalities and memories. It is great that this record of the Five Nations has been produced, and it is a privilege to write these few words.

> "Dublin and Lansdowne Road stood out for me – many a good win and many a good night was had."

*Willie John McBride –
an imposing figure on
the rugby field who
was held in great
respect by opponents
and team-mates alike*

*Willie John McBride
August 1999*

The final five Nations

Richard Cockerill's diary
reveals the inside view of
the 1999 Championship

Garforth, Cockerill and
Leonard in harmony.
In the words of Wellington:
"I don't know what effect
they'll have on the enemy but,
by God, they frighten me…"

The Agony and the Ecstasy

Richard Cockerill's diary of the historic 1999 Five Nations Championship

England hooker Richard Cockerill kept a match-by-match diary of the last Five Nations. His team started the season as favourites, along with France. But Scotland, Wales and Ireland were determined not to let the big two have it all their own way...

"We may not win the title but I think it will be one of the best Five Nations Championships for years."

WALES CAPTAIN
ROB HOWLEY
tries to be positive

Darren Garforth and Richard Cockerill take on the Rhino scrum machine. Opposite: England's unholy trinity of Garforth, Cockerill and Leonard limber up for the 1999 Five Nations

THE BUILD-UP

Ever since England beat the Springboks in December, we've been meeting up on alternate Mondays to keep ourselves focused and make sure we remember our calls. That way, when we get together for the Scotland game we won't have to waste time re-educating ourselves, we can just go straight back into it. The main difference between club and international level is that you have to think faster. It helps that Darren Garforth and I play alongside one another at Leicester, but if you're a good enough player to get picked for your country, then you should be able to adapt to playing with anyone.

In some ways it's harder scrummaging when you practise than when you play – there's a greater pain barrier to go through. When we practise scrummaging with England, we've got this sort of horrible little sled that the forwards coach John Mitchell brought with him from New Zealand. It's a machine of torture. It has minimal padding, lots of sandbags and people standing on it, and when you do 50 or 60 scrums

> **"I believe this will be one of the most open championships for years because all the countries involved have improved out of sight."**
> ENGLAND COACH CLIVE WOODWARD talks down his side's chances

against that, it's pretty painful to be honest. You grind yourself into the floor in training and hope that it pays off in the match.

I'm looking forward to playing in the final Five Nations Championship. Last year it seemed like it was dead and buried. England beat Wales by 60 points and people were saying, 'Is the Five Nations only about England and France?' But this year the Celts all think they're in with a good chance, which is good for the competition. A lot of history goes

> **"The French team is capable of winning the 1999 championship and I believe we will do so."**
> FRANCE COACH JEAN-CLAUDE SKRELA looks ahead wth confidence

with this tournament. It means a lot to all the players. When you're a kid growing up watching the game, playing in the Five Nations is a big ambition and I'm fortunate enough to have played in it. It is special.

THE FIRST WEEKEND

"Whatever happened to the luck of the Irish?"
JONATHAN DAVIES
on Ireland's last-gasp defeat by France

England aren't playing this weekend, so it's a strange way to begin a tournament. In a way it's not actually a Five Nations weekend for us. We aren't due to meet up as a whole squad until just before the Scotland game, and I can't even see the opening games live because Leicester are playing Harlequins in the Premiership. But every Five Nations game is analysed by the coaches, who then send each player a video highlighting their particular area. Our first game is against Scotland, so I'll be watching the scrums and lineouts in that one especially closely.

Saturday 6th February
IRELAND 9 FRANCE 10

Last year's wooden spoon winners entertain the Grand Slam winners – and very nearly beat them. Buoyed by Ulster's victory over Colomiers in the previous weekend's European Cup Final, Ireland lead 9-0 until midway through the second half, when a ragged French team score the only try of the game. A minute from full-time, Thomas Castaignède kicks a penalty to put France one point ahead. Then, two minutes into injury time, David Humphreys has a chance to win the match with a penalty kick 15 metres from the left touchline on the French 22. He misses.

Watching the video of the first game, I couldn't help laughing at the colour of Keith Wood's head. Within three minutes it was completely blue. We always have things painted on the pitch for club games, and it does come off a bit, but never like that.

The French don't travel particularly well and Ireland, in a one-off game, are always a hard side, particularly at Lansdowne Road. But I thought the French would beat them relatively comfortably, so when I heard the score I thought, 'God, that's a fair old effort'. And Ireland really should have won the game with

"It will be raining sunshine in Paris tonight."
FRANCE MANAGER JO MASO
after his side weathered the Irish storm

the last kick. People suggest we might have wanted Ireland to win because France are our biggest rivals. But this year I reckon any of the teams can beat the others. We'll just concentrate on our own game and not worry about who wins the other matches, because if we win all our games we'll win the championship.

"I'm absolutely gutted. I feel like I've been run over by a train. I thought I hit it well but it just fell away from the uprights. We didn't deserve this defeat."
DAVID HUMPHREYS

Vive les Bleus! – Castaignède, top, celebrates as France even turn the Irish players blue with victory at Lansdowne Road, despite a barnstorming display by the home skipper Dion O'Cuinneagain, right

Hanging on for dear life — another Scotsman encounters the difficulties of tackling Scott Gibbs

> "We are good enough to win the Grand Slam."
>
> ALLAN BATEMAN shows the problems with prophecy

Saturday 6th February
SCOTLAND 33 WALES 20

Scotland have been everyone's pre-tournament wooden spoon favourites, while Wales are seen as the pick of the Celts. Yet, in a match of astonishing cut and thrust, Scotland score four tries to Wales's two. They also set a world record with a try after just nine seconds as John Leslie grabs Duncan Hodge's reverse kick-off and saunters over. Gregor Townsend adds a 60-yard breakaway try, while scrum-half Gary Armstrong and lock Scott Murray provide the drive that nullifies Neil Jenkins's kicking power. But Wales still think they have the upper hand until the Scots score 18 points in the last 18 minutes.

The Scotland-Wales result is a surprise, because Scotland were well beaten 35-10 by the South Africans in November, whereas Wales gave the Springboks a big fright and only lost 28-20. So you had to make Wales the favourites, even though they were playing away from home. Seeing Scotland score a try within ten seconds of the kick-off was amazing, even though it was by a New Zealander. But Wales remain a very dangerous team, and with Ireland narrowly losing to France, it looks a very open tournament.

Now that Scotland have won their opening game, their confidence will be high. They are already up to speed, whereas we haven't played yet, so it's going to be a difficult opening game for us. The Scots forwards are very well drilled. The coach Jim Telfer's no mug, as we've seen from the Scotland packs that he's produced before and his work with the Lions.

The pressure is on the England team to carry on the progress we made in the autumn match against South Africa. That's something we failed to do last year when we drew with the All Blacks but then lost to France in the first game of the Five Nations. We're know we mustn't let Scotland beat us. We need a good performance.

> "We had 15 guys who wanted to win more than they did. We had a meritocracy rather than a few idols."
>
> SCOTLAND COACH JIM TELFER reveals the key to victory over Wales

THE SECOND WEEKEND

England's newest star, Jonny Wilkinson, made the difference with his superb kicking as Scotland were edged out at Twickenham

The press has been full of 19-year-old Jonny Wilkinson. I toured with Jonny in the summer and he didn't have a great time. Physically he was intimidated, and he was probably a bit naïve. But this year, with Newcastle, he has blossomed. He has kicked very well at goal and out of hand, and he's confident without being arrogant. He's keen to learn, and a very hard worker.

We meet at the Petersham Hotel at lunchtime on the Tuesday and then we're together until Saturday. We do a couple of training sessions at the Bank of England ground at Roehampton, just across Richmond Park, and a couple at Twickenham. Everyone stays at the hotel, but in the evenings some of the local lads go to see their families or girlfriends. Some of us watch videos of the opposition. If a guy is carrying a knock he'll see the physio. Most of the lads don't like to be distracted too much. They just want to think about the game and get themselves in the frame of mind where they're ready to play.

On the Friday we have a team run in the morning, then it's free in the afternoon. We meet up at seven o'clock for a final pep talk from the captain before dinner. On Saturday, the forwards meet at about 11 o'clock and do 15 minutes of lineouts in the car park. Meanwhile, the backs have a meeting and a chat. I don't know what they talk about – probably what they're going to do after the game...

After the lineouts we have a quick team meeting to remind ourselves what we want to do during the game. At midday we assemble in the hotel meeting room, Clive Woodward says a few words and then we get on the bus to Twickenham.

Clive is a very passionate, off-the-cuff sort of person. He's not much of a pre-planned speech-maker, he just seems to say whatever comes into his mind, which is good. He lives for the moment. He wants passion from his players and the game played with your heart on your sleeve. Anyway, by Saturday morning, his job's done.

There is still a great rivalry over the Calcutta Cup. I found it amazing last year, when we played in Edinburgh, how much the Scots hate the English, for whatever historical reasons. Scotland use it as a big motivational part of their game.

Saturday 20th February
ENGLAND 24 SCOTLAND 21

England's back row set up a 14-0 lead, with Tim Rodber scoring a try and Neil Back putting winger Dan Luger in. But then the home team relax – and against the adventurous Scots that nearly proves fatal. Gregor Townsend scores a breakaway try, and Alan Tait adds two touchdowns. If Kenny Logan had kicked anywhere near as well as Jonny Wilkinson, the scoreline would have looked very different.

We were very conscious that we needed to start well, unlike last year in the French game when we just sort

of turned up and expected things to happen. We got a 14-point lead, but then we sat back and simply didn't play. Trying to sit on a lead at that level is criminal.

Their first try came from a bad lineout ball which they got hold of and eventually Scott Murray managed to give the scoring pass to Alan Tait, who brought them back into the game.

That lifted them and they started to play some really good stuff. Our set-piece scrummaging was quite good, but we didn't take control. When they slowed the ball down, we tended to give it to Catty to do something with instead of taking responsibility for it the way we had practised in training.

Before the game we had set a target of no tries scored against us, but we let three in. We had managed to keep Australia and South Africa to one try – and then we let Scotland get three. Mentally we were just not on top of our game defensively and we got punished for it.

There was a bit of banter in the papers before the game between Alan Tait and Jerry Guscott, so that added a bit of spice to it. But Tait played well and took his tries very well, even though they were more down to our lack of defence than anything else. But at least we dogged it out and got the victory.

If Scotland had won the game by three points everyone would have said that's fantastic, but England have set their stall out to try to win the World Cup and when you don't reach those standards, you're going to get stick.

Saturday 20th February
WALES 23 IRELAND 29

Another upset for Wales at Wembley. David Humphreys charges down a Neil Jenkins clearance for centre Kevin Maggs to score, then hooker Keith Wood waltzes in for a great try as Ireland rack up a 26-6 lead. Converted tries by Craig Quinnell and Shane Howarth restore Welsh respectability, but Humphreys has the last word with a drop-goal.

I had to smile when I saw Keith Wood side-stepping Scott Gibbs to score under the posts. There's obviously rivalry between us on the pitch, but to

be honest, the other hookers I play against are all good guys. The only one I don't get on with is Mark Regan. Apart from that I'm friendly with all the hookers around the world – even Norm Hewitt, the All Black.

Woody is the talisman of Irish rugby, so people do compare our fieriness and our passion for the game. But we're different. He's more

of a loose player who likes to carry the ball up, like a back-rower in some ways. I'm more of a tight player – scrummage, lineout, ruck and maul – which is what England are looking for out of their front row. I'm just a cog that makes everything else work. I do a lot of stuff that people don't see. We have other guys in our pack to do the job Wood does.

> **"We are out of the Five Nations, so the pressure is off. We just have to have a positive attitude going into the England and France matches."**
>
> WALES COACH GRAHAM HENRY after successive defeats in his first two Championship matches

From Maggs to riches – Ireland bounced back with a victory over Wales thanks to a try by Kevin Maggs, though both sets of fans contributed to the Wembley atmosphere

THE THIRD WEEKEND

Mr Muscles, Scott
Quinnell, top, enjoyed
Wales's Paris win in which
Colin Charvis stretched
over for a try, top right.
Meanwhile, Cockerill,
below, and Luger, far
right, were helping
England beat Ireland

Going back to your club between Five Nations matches can be quite difficult. With England you get all the pressure and the tension, and it's all very high profile – and then when you go back to your club, they've all been sat there waiting for you for a week. The coaches aren't particularly interested in what we've done with England. They're eager to get us back on the treadmill, ready for the Leicester roadshow.

It's hard to get yourself back down to earth. Most of our boys at Leicester have been there before, so we've got experience at getting on with it. That's when you show your professional outlook. The Monday you go back to Leicester, that's when you earn your money.

Every game is tough these days. There's not many non-international hookers in the Premiership. In the space of four weeks I'll have played against Gordon Bulloch of Scotland, Wales's Barry Williams, Keith Wood, Argentina's Federico Mendez and Raphael Ibanez of France. You face world-class players week in, week out.

When you're playing for your club, you have to ignore the fact that you may be up against your England colleagues – and that one of you may get hurt. We were playing Northampton recently and it got a little fiery at times. I had to forget that on Tuesday I would be meeting up with Tim Rodber and Matt Dawson and we'd be on the same side. What happens on the pitch stays on the pitch.

This weekend our Five Nations opponents are Ireland. When we arrive in Dublin, Clive has a meeting with the forwards and tells us: "Either you do the business in this game or it might be the last you get." He wasn't particularly pleased with the forwards' performance against Scotland, and there are a few harsh words. The pressure is on for us all.

"People should be judged on their ability to play. People who watch me play rugby may think I'm thick or a thug, but when they talk to me they are surprised that I come across as articulate and intelligent. Rugby is a confrontational sport and that means getting in your opponent's face. Sledging is a part of that for me, just as it is for someone like Sean Fitzpatrick. Some of us can talk and play at the same time."

RICHARD COCKERILL
strikes a blow for hookers
everywhere

International rugby is a very competitive business and you don't get too many bites of the cherry. You are there to do a job for your country, and if you're not doing it, there's plenty of people queueing up to have a go.

Ireland have already beaten Wales and only just lost to France, and people are starting to say they could win the Triple Crown. England have not had great away form in Dublin, so everybody seems to be expecting us to get turned over. That will get us well motivated!

The England squad are trained not to give the newspapers any quotes that can be put into headlines to motivate other sides. Before the Scotland game, after they had beaten Wales, the management showed us cuttings with Gregor Townsend saying that Scotland can win the Grand Slam. That's quite a motivational thing. Now Ireland's Kiwi coach Warren Gatland is saying they've got the best tight five in the championship. Maybe it's his idea of psychological

warfare, but it just works the opposite way. I'd rather have them slagging us off any time. John Mitchell has been winding us up, saying: "Cockerill, they don't rate you, mate. They don't think you're good enough." These things get to you. You either bottle it or stand up and be counted. This is going to be a big challenge for us.

Saturday 6th March
IRELAND 15 ENGLAND 27

The England forwards respond to Irish taunts by camping in the enemy's half and refusing to budge. Ireland stay in touch on the scoreboard until the last quarter thanks to five penalties by David Humphreys, but England hammer out a convincing win with tries by Matt Perry and Tim Rodber, a drop-goal by Paul Grayson and 14 points from kicker Jonny Wilkinson.

Before the match, Clive showed us a another cutting in the English press saying that if we lost in Dublin, his perception of how the game should be played would be conceptually flawed and his big-name players would be proved gutless. If we had lost, we would have been crucified – and I don't think there would have been many of the front five remaining in the side. At this level when the pressure's on, as it was in Dublin, you've got to come up with the goods and fortunately we did.

There's a very passionate crowd in Dublin and it's real backs-to-the-wall stuff. It's easy to talk about things in the press and say what you're going to do, but when you're actually out there on the pitch you must stand up and be counted. All the players from one to 15 did that. The crowd can boo us and abuse us, but it just makes you even more determined to beat them. It's nice to see the crowd start to walk off with two or three minutes to go, because they know they've lost. That's encouraging from an English point of view. We've had a tough start to the final Five Nations and fortunately we've come through unbeaten.

Saturday 6th March
FRANCE 33 WALES 34

Wales's first win in Paris since 1975 is the stuff of legend. They match the French, for whom Emile Ntamack scores a hat-trick of tries, with an expansive running game. There are three Welsh tries – by Colin Charvis, Dafydd James and Craig Quinnell – and although Neil Jenkins misses four penalties in a row, Wales reach full-time one point ahead. Then Thomas Castaignède misses a penalty in injury time, and Wales can celebrate a breathless victory.

The France-Wales game started just before ours. They showed it on the big screen at Lansdowne Road as we warmed up, and I could vaguely see both sides had scored over 30 points. I couldn't believe Wales had done that, but we had enough on our plate without watching TV. When they told us the result at half-time, I was astonished. Afterwards, we watched it on the video before our dinner. The Welsh played exceptionally well. Both sides attacked brilliantly – but then both defended really badly.

> **"They can talk the talk, but they didn't walk the walk, did they?"**
> RICHARD COCKERILL
> after England's victory over Ireland

> **"The best performance since I've been coach."**
> CLIVE WOODWARD
> satisfied with victory

THE FOURTH WEEKEND

Kicking into history – Wilkinson, top right, and Humphreys, top, were crucial points scorers in 1999 whatever the efforts of forwards like Martin Corry, right, Andy Ward, opposite top, and backs like Gregor Townsend, far right

So, France next, and we're all feeling pretty nervous about it. Ever since they lost to Wales, Thomas Castaignède has been saying that the English will pay for that result when we meet them at Twickenham. Last year they beat us quite convincingly, so the boys don't really know what to expect. The French can either be really poor or absolutely out of this world. Which mood will they be in on Saturday?

Saturday 20th March
ENGLAND 21 FRANCE 10

The French are blown away by the ferocious power of the English forwards, who pulverise the opposition into submission while boy wonder Jonny Wilkinson fires an England record of seven penalties out of seven. It is 21-3 to the home side at full-time and a try four minutes into injury time by Franck Comba cannot spare the blushes of dispirited France.

To be fair, we had pretty much total control from the start. We scrummaged very well, our lineout worked superbly, and the French were very ill-disciplined and gave lots of penalties away. And obviously Jonny was on top form with his kicking. He made all his attempts – which we got criticised about because we didn't run it enough, apparently; but when you've got points sitting there waiting to be kicked you've got to take them.

The French seem to be suffering from a total lack of confidence. They were arguing with each other, there was simply no team spirit. When

things went against them they just disintegrated, which is surprising. We expected them to be more fiery and physical, because French forwards are usually quite abrasive.

It was 21-3 at one point – and we'd missed several try-scoring chances as well. Mike Catt perhaps should have scored in the first half when he had a two-man overlap and tried to make the line himself and got caught just short. Jerry Guscott dropped the ball over the line. So we could have had 30 or 40 points.

There was a strange mood in the dressing room afterwards. We were a bit dissatisfied because we'd played well and if we'd scored some tries, that would have finished it off. We set ourselves high standards because we want to be a major force in the World Cup, and if you're going to do that you need to take your chances.

> **"It is not a false dawn, it's a little bit of sunshine peeking through."**
> SCOTLAND COACH
> JIM TELFER
> spies light at the end of the tunnel

Saturday 20th March
SCOTLAND 30 IRELAND 13

Ireland's season, which started so promisingly, ends in disappointment, while Scotland, under Gregor Townsend's prompting, soar ever higher. A penalty try for Ireland after two minutes merely serves to set the Scots' adrenalin pumping. Townsend scores his now usual try, and Cameron Murray grabs two as he and Stuart Grimes both score in the first two minutes of the second half.

Yet again Scotland took everyone by surprise. After Ireland's performances against the French and the Welsh, I thought they would win it. But the Scots have managed to perform week in, week out, rather than just raising themselves for the odd game like they used to do. Suddenly it begins to look as if they could beat France in Paris. Obviously we would like to see the French win that game. But now the Scots will go there full of confidence. Their key player is Gregor Townsend, who's very much a confidence player, and if he's confident and on top of his game, he's very dangerous.

Meanwhile, there's a strange score from Treviso – Italy 21 Wales 60, with seven Welsh tries. The squad were amazed. But then we watched the game and to be honest the Italians didn't play particularly well, giving away quite a few soft tries. Some of the Italians are predicting Wales will beat us at Wembley. We'll see…

> **"Kenny Logan has had a go at me because he has played about five times as many Five Nations matches as me but has never scored. He was unmarked outside me but I had my blinkers on and I just went straight to the line."**
> SCOTLAND LOCK STUART GRIMES
> after scoring the try described as the most spectacular ever at Murrayfield

THE FINAL WEEKEND

"We ripped them to shreds."

SCOTLAND CAPTAIN
GARY ARMSTRONG
on his side's win in Paris

Up the Glenn – Scotland were well served in their title victory by full back Glenn Metcalfe, top, lock Scott Murray, and flanker Martin Leslie, who scored in Paris, far right

We meet up at the Petersham Hotel in Richmond as usual on the Tuesday, even though the game's not until Sunday. Suddenly we're hit by a spate of injuries, and David Rees and Jeremy Guscott are both forced to pull out. Clive brings in two new caps, which causes one supporter to complain to me that every time he opens the paper there's another England player he's never heard of. People assume it must be unsettling, but to be honest we don't give a lot of thought to it. When players are injured, Clive's pretty relaxed about it. The attitude is: OK, they're injured, Barrie-Jon Mather is playing, Steve Hanley's playing, these guys are here on merit, let's get on with it.

Steve Hanley has been playing outstandingly well for Sale, and Barrie-Jon Mather has a very good reputation from his rugby league days. It's obviously disappointing to lose people of Rees's and Jerry's class, but there's no point moping about it, you've just got to do the job.

The only worry is that there's not a lot of experience among the backs – Dan Luger and Jonny Wilkinson aren't exactly old hands yet. It's also very difficult for Steve and Barrie-Jon to be making their debuts in such a massive game. But if Clive thinks someone's good enough, whether they're 17 or 37, he'll select them. He picks from a gut feeling about people, and 99 per cent of the time his gut feeling is pretty good. The press have

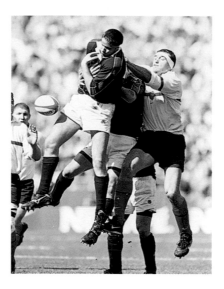

"The first half was unbelievable. Everything we had worked on in training seemed to come off. It was one of the most enterprising Scottish performances for a long, long time. We could have scored four or five more tries. I was trying to call them to kick the ball at times, but they just wouldn't."

SCOTLAND COACH JIM TELFER
struggles to contain his delight

been comparing Steve Hanley to Jonah Lomu. He's big, quick and skilful, but I think to say that about a lad who's only 19 making his Test debut is a bit premature.

That's a lot of pressure for a young guy who was playing for Aspatria in the fourth division only a year ago.

The greatest threat from Wales will be the speed at which they play the game. It's quite high-risk. Scott Gibbs, the Quinnell brothers and Chris Wyatt are all very mobile, and big people to have to knock down all the time. Then obviously there's Neil Jenkins with his kicking ability…

Of course, the possibility of an England Grand Slam adds extra pressure. If you say you're not thinking about it, you'd be lying. To beat Wales would be a great achievement in itself. But to beat Wales and win the Grand Slam would be fantastic. So, yeah, the pressure's on – but pressure's a good thing, especially for this English side. The games in which we've really produced the goods have been the ones when we've been most under pressure.

Saturday 10th April
FRANCE 22 SCOTLAND 36

Scotland coach Jim Telfer's last Five Nations match is also his best. In one of the most amazing games ever staged in the championship's history, 52 points are scored in the first 27 minutes, 33 of them by Scotland. And all this after Thomas Castaignède had laid on a try for Emile Ntamack in the first minute. But while Castaignède limps off injured immediately after that, opposing fly half Gregor Townsend orchestrates the most exhilarating display of running rugby ever seen from a Scottish team. Townsend runs in a try himself to become only the fifth man ever to score tries in all matches of a Five Nations season, and Alan Tait matches Ntamack by

scoring his fifth of the tournament as the Scots score five tries to France's three. Now Scotland have to hope that Wales win at Wembley the next day to deny England the title.

I watched the France-Scotland game on the big screen in the hotel with a few of the lads. Some of the other guys had gone into town to get away from rugby for a few hours – they missed a great game and an almost unbelievable first half.

When France scored after a minute we thought, great, but then Castaignède went off, with scrum half Philippe Carbonneau following before half-time, and from an English viewpoint it went downhill from

there. The preliminaries were hilarious, with the band playing Flower of Scotland really slowly, just to wind the Scots up.

Jim Telfer had been saying: "We need to get a good start because once the French get their tails up, they'll be really into the game and we'll struggle." So when the French scored after a minute, I thought, now we'll see what Scotland are made of. They could have just folded, but to their credit

> **"I have been lucky enough to play for some really great teams in both codes, but this is definitely the best Scotland team I have played for."**
> ALAN TAIT
> rates his victorious colleagues

they hit straight back and went on to score five tries before half-time. I think Castaignède going off was a big turning point, because he had cut them to shreds. But the Scots did very, very well, and coped brilliantly with all the noise and the pressure and the hostile atmosphere.

It was frustrating for us watching, because obviously if the French had beaten them, we'd already have the championship. But at the end of the day we want to beat Wales regardless of the Scottish result, because we want to win the Grand Slam. We don't want to rely on somebody else's results. We want to win it ourselves, by right.

Seeing Scotland running tries in almost at will was really strange, as it was only a year since that French side had won the championship quite convincingly. But this year their basics of defence and organisation have been completely missing. They were pretty shocking. The Scots were outstanding, though. They create lots of chances and against the French they took the majority of them.

So it's a little bit disappointing for the English. But from a Scottish point of view it was a fantastic win – and for the Five Nations it was good as it leaves everything hanging on tomorrow's final match between Wales and England. Now the pressure really is on...

> **"I was excited when I ran over the line. I had thought about it earlier in the week but didn't want to count on anything."**
> GREGOR TOWNSEND
> after becoming only the fifth man to score in every match of a Five Nations season

> **"It was simply an extraordinary way for Saturdays in the Five Nations to vanish for ever."**
> EDDIE BUTLER
> in *The Observer*

THE FINAL GAME

"I have never seen a kicking display better than that. If the posts had been two metres apart instead of 10, Neil Jenkins would still have kicked all his points."
WALES COACH
GRAHAM HENRY

The last Five Nations game will be the most important Five Nations game ever for me and a lot of the other England players. It's a four o'clock kick-off at Wembley, which makes it different from a normal away game because obviously you're training at home. And it will be nice to say you've played at the home of English football.

The feeling in the changing room is good. We've prepared and trained well. The boys are up for the game.

We go out on the pitch and get some stick from the Welsh supporters and a lot of cheering from the English. The Welsh are out-shouting the English quite easily – it feels more like we're in Wales than England. The Welsh are very passionate about their rugby and they've turned up to support their team come what may. It's a fantastic atmosphere. Great stadium, lovely surface. A great day to clinch a Grand Slam and we're all confident we can do it…

Sunday 11th April
WALES 32 ENGLAND 31
Scott Gibbs and Neil Jenkins bring about the most dramatic ending possible to a Five Nations tournament as, two minutes into injury time, Gibbs scythes through the entire English defence to score a sensational try, leaving 'Jenkins the Boot' to convert and knock the Grand Slam from England's grasp. Starting with Dan Luger's try in the third minute, England had dominated, with Wales hanging on thanks to eight Jenkins penalties. The crucial moment comes in the 76th minute when

Oh boyo, was it a trying time for England at Wembley as Scott Gibbs, celebrating top, crashed over in the last minute to cancel out an early score by Dan Luger, right, and confirm the rampaging work of Craig Quinnell, far right

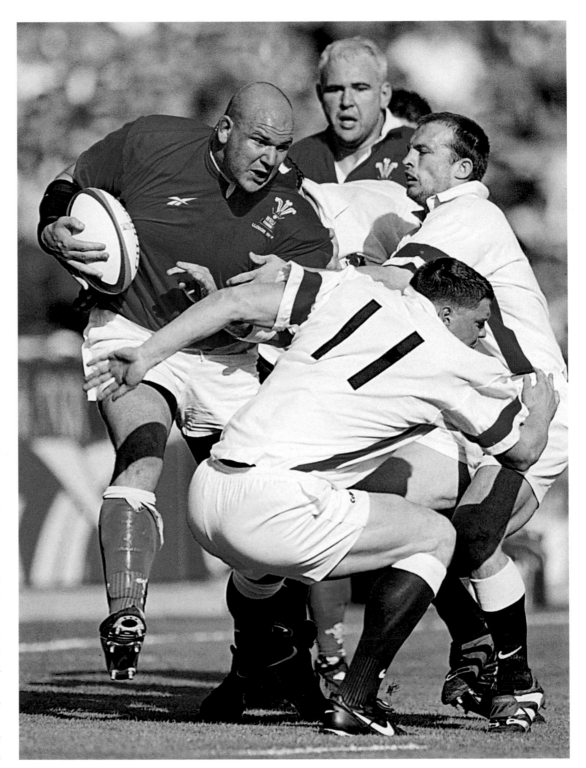

England captain Lawrence Dallaglio opts for position from a kickable penalty rather than the points which would secure a nine-point lead. With the door left open, Gibbs and Jenkins make England pay dearly.

The result didn't reflect the way we prepared because we prepared very, very well. We started superbly, with a try after three minutes. We broke down the middle, Matt Perry put Dan Luger away and off he went. It was a great start, and we just wanted to get back and make sure we didn't concede any points straight away. But every time we kicked off we never really cleared our own lines. We played a lot of the game in our own half and kept giving penalties away, which Jenks kicked easily.

Wales played very well. They didn't let us take complete control and in the end it cost us dear. We were good enough to beat them but we weren't as clinical as we should have been. It's frustrating, but we've got to realise that you can't sit on a lead of six points and run the clock down, you've got to keep playing the same way. We got in the lead by running the ball and taking them on, and we scored some good tries, but we should have done that all through the game – especially in the latter stages.

Otherwise you get to 80 minutes, 81, 82 minutes, you've been in the lead all through the game – and then they manage to sneak it. It's a valuable lesson for us that we don't want to repeat.

After Luger's try, Jenkins brought Wales back into the game with a

"We are shattered. There is not a lot I can say to the players because the selections were right, the tactics were right, but we lost the game."

CLIVE WOODWARD
just can't believe it

Debutant Steve Hanley scored a try, below, but Dawson, Cockerill and Luger were dancing to different tunes, right. Neil Jenkins, opposite, had a profound effect on the final scoreline, and it left Howarth and Sinkinson, far right, celebrating the win

couple of penalties, but then we built a six-point lead when Hanley scored a try in the 21st minute after we kicked a penalty to the corner and had a three-man lineout. It was a set move: the three men went back, I threw it to Tim Rodber coming at the front, he gave it back to me and after a couple of phases we stretched their defence and Steve came on a good line to score his debut try. Jonny Wilkinson surprisingly missed the conversion. If he'd got that, perhaps we'd have won, but you can't be perfect every day.

Just before half-time Wales had a mix-up and Richard Hill snaffled the ball for a soft try. We were 10 points ahead then, and we said let's make sure we don't give any penalties away before half-time, as that would have meant they needed two scores to get back into it. And of course they kicked off and we gave another penalty away, which Jenkins kicked.

It was very frustrating because we had run them ragged. Then we got off to a shocking start in the second half when Neil Back knocked on and gave them a scrum about 10 yards out that they scored from. That put them level at 25-25 and back in the game. If we'd scored first in the second half, it would probably have killed them off.

"When Scott scored his try, everyone was jumping up and down – but we were still a point behind on the scoreboard so I knew it was a conversion I couldn't miss. I blanked out the 79,000 crowd and imagined I was on the local park."

NEIL JENKINS
makes his winning kick sound easy

But they grew in strength, though we never felt under much threat. We felt confident we were going to win.

But we kept giving away penalties – and that's how the Gibbs try came. They were counter-attacking and Tim Rodber put in a big hit on Colin Charvis. The referee said it was fine but the touch judge ruled it a shoulder barge – which on the TV you can see it wasn't. But they got the penalty and kicked it up to the 22 for a short lineout. Wyatt tapped it off the top to Scott Quinnell, who fed Gibbs on a good line to leave our defence flat-footed. He stepped past Matt Perry and in he went. It was a good move but we should be able to defend things like that. He just ran straight through a crowd of players.

There was no way Neil Jenkins was going to miss the conversion, but there were still three or four minutes left, so, behind the posts, we said: "We're still in this. It's our kick-off, let's get in there." And we could have won the game but Catty fluffed his drop goal attempt and that was that.

When the whistle went I was gutted. There was a lot of noise, with all the Wales players going mad. It was a great disappointment, but I believe you take the credit when you win, and when you lose you shake hands and say "Well done", and walk off with your head held high. In the dressing room the boys were shattered because we had given the game away. It was a terrible feeling.

If I was a neutral fan, I would think it was a great Five Nations. People were saying after 1998 that it wasn't worth playing because it was too one-sided, but in 1999 that has been proved wrong. From a pure rugby point of view it has been a brilliant championship. I'll always be proud to have played in the last Five Nations Championship. They say in the history of the Five Nations, this one was the best – but for me, right now, it feels like the worst.

> "The crowd at Twickenham could learn something from the one at Wembley. Noise like that makes such a difference to the players."
> AUSTIN HEALEY
> after the defeat by Wales

> "When I wake up in the morning I still won't believe we lost this game."
> CLIVE WOODWARD
> finds defeat hard to take

> "I don't think they showed us respect as a team – but I think they will respect us now."
> GRAHAM HENRY
> has a lesson for England

THE REACTION

At the end of the last Five Nations Championship, a tournament that went down to the very last kick, Scotland surprised themselves and their fans by finishing as champions. It was undoubtedly one of the most sensational Five Nations ever. Here are the final verdicts...

SCOTTISH REACTION

"It's heavier than the wooden spoon."
GARY ARMSTRONG says it all after lifting the Five Nations Trophy

"At the start of the season Scottish rugby was in disarray. For us to come out on top is nothing short of a miracle."
FORMER SCOTLAND CAPTAIN SCOTT HASTINGS

"The drama of the whole weekend was like a wonderful opera which came to an amazing climax. It was almost as if we were fated to win it."
SCOTLAND COACH JIM TELFER

"I had kind of given up by half-time because I thought England were going to walk it."
GARY ARMSTRONG is glad to be proved wrong

"I rarely get emotional, but when Neil Jenkins had that last kick I was watching and saying, 'Please get one more over'. This Championship was almost as good as Durban when the Lions beat South Africa. This is one of the great days. On Saturday we won a game. Yesterday we won a Championship."
JIM TELFER can hardly believe his side's achievement

"Though Neil Jenkins was outstanding, Gregor Townsend was by far the best No 10 in the Championship. Townsend, John Leslie and second-row Scott Murray were probably the players of the Championship."
NORTHAMPTON AND ex-LIONS COACH IAN MCGEECHAN

Triumphant Scots – Gary Armstrong, top; coach Jim Telfer, taking a pinch of the Saltire Cross; Gregor Townsend, John Leslie and Scott Murray, bottom left to right. Leslie's running, far right, was a key element

THE SOUTHERN
HEMISPHERE VERDICT

"I've been very
impressed with the
Five Nations
Championship.
Scotland and Wales in
particular have
renewed my faith in
running rugby in the
northern hemisphere."
ZINZAN BROOKE
FORMER ALL BLACKS No8

"This tournament is
huge, bigger than
anything I expected."
WALES'S NEW ZEALAND-BORN
COACH GRAHAM HENRY

"I was enthralled with
what I saw this
weekend. And if any of
the so-called super
powers of the southern
hemisphere think they
are going to breeze
past these teams in
the World Cup, they
had better book early
flights home."
FORMER AUSTRALIAN FLY HALF
MICHAEL LYNAGH

"John is the sort of
player who makes a
fly half feel good
about himself just
by being there.
He never hides and
he never drops you
in it. He's always
desperate for the
ball, which suits
me fine because
I always want to
do something with
the ball once
we've won it."
GREGOR TOWNSEND
on Scotland's
New Zealand-born
centre John Leslie

Wales

Think Five Nations, and you think of Wales. The kings of the 1970s were everybody's heroes as they jinked and sidestepped their way into the hearts of rugby fans the world over. It is a reputation which will never be diminished

Passionate and vocal – and that's before their team run out on the pitch – Welsh fans brought up on glory demand success from their team

WRU

BY
IEUAN EVANS

The try master: Evans, opposite, scored on his Five Nations debut

'If Wales came second it was a disastrous year'

Ieuan Evans is Wales' most-capped player with 72 appearances, of which 35 were in the Five Nations. Ieuan captained Wales a record 28 times, and took them to the title in 1994. His record of 33 tries puts him 13 ahead of his two greatest heroes, Gareth Edwards and Gerald Davies. But, as he says here, the legend of the Seventies dragon still looms large...

My earliest memory of a major match wasn't in the Five Nations, but it did involve one of the best Five Nations sides ever put together. The first international I ever went to was the 1973 Barbarians-All Blacks game. I remember that there was a glut of tickets before the BaaBaas line-up was announced, because no one thought it would be a very good side. As soon as the team was known, everyone clamoured for tickets, but somehow I managed to get one – albeit in a different part of the stand from where my father was.

So there I was at the age of nine sat on my own in the North Stand at Cardiff Arms Park watching this spectacle. That Barbarians line-up included nearly half of the Wales team – John Dawes, JPR, Gareth Edwards, Derek Quinnell, Tommy David, Phil Bennett – and they all had a hand in Gareth's legendary try. Hell of a start to a game. But I missed it because everybody stood up and I couldn't see!

I had been brought up on a diet of rugby. My father used to coach the local youth side, so rugby was very much part of my life. I was spoilt, really. I grew up to expect that Wales would always be competing for either a Grand Slam or a Triple Crown, and if they came second it was a disastrous year. But later it became a bit of a millstone at times. When you have to accomplish the same endeavours as your heroes and your father's heroes before that, it can put quite a pressure on your shoulders.

The year I was called up, 1987, the first game of the Five Nations season was to be Ireland at Cardiff, but it was postponed due to bad weather. So my first match ended up being in France at Parc des Princes, which is a fair cauldron to go and receive your first cap. It was the first time I had been to play at Parc des Princes, and as far as I was concerned it was over before it started. One minute I was running out, the next minute I was coming off. It was a game we should have won, but after Paul Thorburn went off injured we missed four or five very kickable penalties and lost 16-9.

It was an exceptional day. Mind you, I practically missed my cap ceremony after the game, because I recognised somebody from Carmarthen in the hotel reception and went for a drink with them. Meanwhile, upstairs they called my name out in front of all the "alakadues" and there was no sign of me. The president stood up and said: "It's a

> "My first Five Nations match seemed to be over before it started: one minute I was running out, the next minute I was coming off."
> IEUAN EVANS
> remembers his debut in 1987

Ieuan Evans scorches his
way to his famous try
against Scotland in 1988

president's greatest honour to bestow caps on new players, so it's my honour to present caps to Kevin Phillips and Ieuan Evans." The applause went up... and no sign of I Evans. I was happily strolling up the stairs minding my own business with a bottle of beer in my hand. I got a very nasty glare from the chairman of selectors and my career was nearly over before it began.

For the next match, against England, we were at home. There's no better feeling than running out for a Five Nations game at Cardiff Arms Park. The buzz of anticipation and then the adrenalin surge are very difficult to replicate. People spend thousands of pounds injecting themselves with God knows what to get the same sort of feeling that I get running out there, and it's all natural. I hope the new stadium captures the same gladiatorial amphitheatre atmosphere as the old Arms Park. It really was unique.

We beat England that year by 19 points to 12. But, win or lose, there's always something special about an England game because it's a David and Goliath scenario – a country of 40 million against a country of three million. For years people would say, "I don't care what we do in the Five Nations as long as we beat England." Thankfully I think we've moved away from that, but it's still the biggest game, no doubt about that, and we'll never get away from that because England are our nearest neighbours and 15 times the size of us. It sometimes felt like that on the pitch, as well, as in my time they always had a superb pack. We've always had gifted backs but the only ball we got was scraps. Sometimes we've been able to survive on scraps and win, which says more for the Welsh character than anything else.

To round off my first Five Nations, I scored a try in the final match against Ireland. So I was looking forward to the 1988 season – and it turned out to be one of the highlights of my Five Nations career. Wales won the Triple Crown and shared the title with France with a side full of good young players just developing their international careers, like Rob Jones, Bleddyn Bowen, Jonathan Davies, Mark Ring, John Devereux, Paul Moriarty and Dai Young. We won at Twickenham 11-3 without much ball, but we still produced two tries through some inspirational play by Jonathan and some great finishing. Whenever we had the ball we had to play with it, as we didn't know when we were going to have another sniff of it, so we were running it from anywhere. It was an exciting time. We were all quite young and we didn't know any different. We should have clinched the Grand Slam, too, but we lost 10-9 to France in Cardiff in the mud.

The best moment of 1988 for me personally came in the game against Scotland at Cardiff, when I scored a try that people often remind me about. It was one of those see-saw games: Scotland got a bit of a lead with a try by Finlay Calder, so we were playing catch-up and whenever we scored, they scored again to keep a gap. Jonathan scored a superb try when he put a grubber kick through the whole of their defence from a reverse pass by Rob Jones and outpaced everybody to score.

My try came towards the end of the first half, from first-phase ball. There were a couple of missed passes and loops involved, and I think Mark Ring looped round to supply Adrian Hadley coming in from the blind side. He offloaded to me and I just kept stepping inside all the time as the cover was coming across. I think I jinked the ref twice. I remember people shouting for the ball off me but I wasn't releasing it for hell or anything. David Sole eventually got me as I scored underneath the posts – that shows how far I came back inside. He had just emerged from the scrum but I keep telling people that he was very, very quick. It was exciting stuff. Unfortunately, the triumphs of that season were somewhat spoilt by the fact that we then went to New Zealand and caught a hiding from the best team I ever played against, losing by 50 points in both Tests.

My other Five Nations highlight was captaining Wales to the championship in 1994, but again it was very much by surviving on scraps. We beat Scotland in the rain playing good handling rugby, we beat Ireland in a very tight game, as it usually is at Lansdowne Road, and we beat France with a good individual performance by Scott Quinnell. We went to Twickenham on a wave of euphoria, as there always is when Wales have some success. Often, expectations build to an extreme level, even on the flimsiest of evidence.

But at Twickenham we buckled under the pressure. There was a lot of Welsh support there that day, but it was an anticlimax because we lost the game. We could have won if we had played as well as in the first three games, but it wasn't to be. It was nice to lift the trophy at Twickenham, but in the photographs there's only a faint smile on my face. We lost the battle but won the war. Even so, that was probably my proudest moment in the Five Nations because we won the trophy for the first time in six years. The Nineties have not been the greatest of times for Welsh rugby and I was part of it for all that time, so maybe I'm the jinx! But I thoroughly enjoyed playing in the Five Nations.

We in the northern hemisphere should be justifiably proud of it. For Wales, it is an opportunity to shine on the world stage. It's the jewel in our crown and for many years it was the envy of the southern hemisphere countries. Recently they've tried to pour scorn on it – but now that Graham Henry has sampled it as Wales coach, he says the intensity of it caught him totally unawares. It is still the prime rugby competition outside of the World Cup. It's a great spectacle and the build-up during the week is very special. That's something we really have to hold on to when it becomes the Six Nations with Italy joining.

The last Five Nations Championship was one of the best. There were so many twists and turns. You might have predicted that England would be competing for a Grand Slam – but not the way that France capitulated; the way that Wales beat England and France but lost to Scotland and Ireland; the way that Scotland were seen as definite wooden spooners and ended up winning the title…

And there was some great rugby: enterprising, 15-man, total rugby. Not quite the way it has gone in the Super 12, with its uncompetitive scrums, but hard-hitting, physical, hard-nosed rugby combined with the ability to score tries. The tries Scotland, Wales and England scored this year had all elements, and it has been one of the great Five Nations. When rugby is played like that it is a beautiful game.

A defining moment for Wales and their fans as Neil Jenkins, top, secures victory against England in the last ever Five Nations game

IEUAN EVANS' ALL-TIME WALES FIVE NATIONS XV

Ieuan Evans had probably the toughest job of our dream team selectors, because Wales is such a land of legends. But, as he pointed out: "Some great players played in poor teams, and they are no lesser players because they haven't had the rewards of Triple Crowns and Grand Slams like the Seventies players." Ieuan stressed that he could only pick from players he could remember – from the Seventies onwards. But he added: "I think it's a decent side. When you're at school you love to try to pick your best Welsh side, but when you actually have to put it down in print, it's different. I'm expecting to take a few phone calls!"

The centres, wings and flankers gave Ieuan some problems but his hardest choice was to pick one fly half from Wales's outstanding candidates. His contemporary Jonathan Davies, top right, got the nod

15 JPR Williams (Full back)
He stands alone. Fifty-five caps, captain of Wales, great deeds for the Lions – JPR Williams was a legend, the outstanding Welsh full back of the past 40 years. This was one of the easiest positions to fill.

14 Gerald Davies (Right wing)
He was my idol. It was Gerald who I aspired to be when I was playing in the back garden with a rubber ball in my hands – him along with Johan Cruyff, but I couldn't fit Cruyff into the team!

13 Allan Bateman (Outside centre)
He's the finest centre I've played with. He's very, very quick, and defensively he is magnificent – he's extremely unselfish, and always communicating with the winger. He'll never take the easy option of taking someone out unnecessarily if he can work hard to get to the next player, and once he gets hold of you it's like a clamp, he won't release. Rugby league made him

a more complete player, and he was very unlucky not to secure a Test berth on the last Lions tour. He's what the modern rugby player is all about: supreme fitness, strength and all-round ability.

12 John Dawes
(Inside centre) Captain
This position gave me more of a problem, but John would also be captain because he was a magnificent leader. He's an out-and-out inside centre and hopefully he and Allan would complement each other. John is more of a footballer, a great passer. Several other names were the frame – Bleddyn Bowen, Steve Fenwick, Ray Gravell, Scott Gibbs and even Mark Ring. But Mark got injured early in his career. If he had carried on, he'd have probably got in as he was the most talented footballer I've ever seen.

11 JJ Williams (Left wing)
This was a choice between Maurice Richards and JJ. I ended up choosing

JJ because I can't remember a lot about Maurice, even though I've often been compared to him. JJ Williams, with the tries he scored on the 1974 Lions tour of South Africa, and his pace and his fitness, was the supreme athlete. You've only got to look at the Graham Price try at Parc des Princes in '75, when he crossed from the opposite wing to get to the ball, to realise the work ethic he had.

10 Jonathan Davies (Outside half)
This was by far the most difficult spot to fill, because it's the one area where Wales have a plethora of players to pick from. It was a toss-up between Barry John and Jonathan Davies, but I'm going to go for Jonathan, probably because I played with him. He played in a poor Welsh side and still stood out, whereas Barry didn't have to suffer in a bad team, and retired very early at 26. If he had played another three or four seasons, he would have waltzed in. Jonathan played on, then went to league and then came back, so

I'm going to go for him. I'll probably get pilloried for it, but I can relate to Jonathan because I played in a struggling Welsh side for most of my career and I know how difficult it is to play on poor ball. His strength of character shone through. He'll be my kicker, too. Jonathan Davies will buy me a drink, but Barry John will probably never speak to me again.

9 Gareth Edwards (Scrum half)

Recently ranked the greatest rugby player who ever lived, and that's what he was – there's no doubt. Modern-day players who may not remember a lot about him should get a video out and take a look. He was what everybody should aspire to be, a complete player – very quick, very strong, a magnificent athlete. He had to work hard on the technicalities of the game (his passing, for example), but he did and he came through. A thorn in any defence, he seemed to score at will, and whenever the big game was on he would pull something out of the bag. Gareth played in the great era for Wales, but even through the torrid times, it's the half backs who have shone. At scrum half you've got people like Terry Holmes, Robert Jones, Rob Howley, but Gareth is just way ahead.

1 Charlie Faulkner (Loosehead prop)

Played in the front row with Price and Windsor for Pontypool and the Lions. But it's their exploits for Wales in the Seventies, when they played 15 Five Nations games in a row and won two Grand Slams and two Triple Crowns, that make them essential to my team.

2 Bobby Windsor (Hooker)

Closely followed by Alan Phillips, but I ended up going for Bobby mainly because I wanted to keep the Viet Gwent together in the front row.

3 Graham Price (Tighthead prop)

He epitomised the way forward for the pack – and for the front row in particular. Modern props have evolved from Graham Price. Fit, very quick and strong, he could scrummage and keep up with play in the loose as well, which is what players have to do today. Back then it was largely unheard of: props scrummaged and that was it.

4 Geoff Wheel (Lock)

He was an immense man at the heart of the pack and the front of the lineout. A good scrummager, he was excellent in the maul – no one got the ball back off him. He was terrifically strong and a great character as well.

5 Robert Norster (Lock)

A gifted athlete, and a superb lineout technician who could handle his own in the loose as well.

6 Jeff Squire (Blindside flanker)
7 John Taylor (Openside flanker)

The flankers caused some consternation. In the end I opted for Jeff and John to get a bit of balance. Jeff Squire on the blind side – he's a stronger man, a bigger man, whereas John Taylor was an out-and-out openside with a good rugby brain and some speed. I wanted to put Dai Morris in there somewhere but Jeff Squire and John Taylor were a better balance.

8 Mervyn Davies (No 8)

A superb leader of men, Merv the Swerve was the stand-out '8' throughout his career. As with Gerald, Gareth and JPR, you wouldn't consider anybody else in their roles.

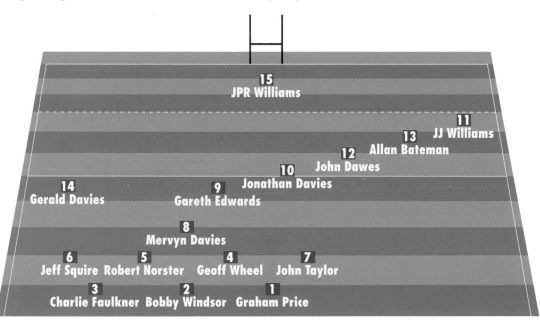

Early Success

England, always the old enemy, may have claimed the title in the debut Five Nations season but the Welsh quickly went one better by securing the championship's first Grand Slam

Wales were the form team through the early 1900s before the International Championship welcomed France as the fifth nation. Between 1900 and 1909 Wales were the best side of the Home Unions on no fewer than five occasions, and although the Welsh finished second behind England in the inaugural Five Nations tournament in 1910, they were flying in 1911.

With 55 tries scored, the 1911 Five Nations Championship was a real feast of rugby. Wales registered 18 of them en route to finishing the championship with the highest points total: 78. That was good enough for them to win the tournament for the first time, and make them the first country ever to achieve a Five Nations Grand Slam.

The season opened against England at Swansea – and it was Wales's toughest match of the series, though they won 15-11. Next up came Scotland in Inverleith, Edinburgh and the eight tries Wales ran in was a record for the country in a match against the Scots. Seven of the eight came courtesy of players attached to Cardiff, the only exception being Pontypool's Rhys Thomas. Scotland were just no match for the rampant Welsh – in fact, 1911 was a miserable year for Scottish fans. Their team lost all four of their games and conceded a total of 19 tries in the process.

Wales's 32-10 in Edinburgh turned the team's thoughts towards the possibility of a Grand Slam. The third game in their series was the country's first championship match in France, and the 15-0 winning margin remained Wales's best victory in Paris until the margin was equalled in a 25-10 win in 1975.

That left Ireland to come to Cardiff Arms Park, with the match a Triple Crown and Grand Slam decider – the winner would take all the spoils. Some 40,000 fans packed into the ground, and thousands more were left outside. They witnessed a Welsh team which was never threatened and eventually ran out 16-0 winners – the first Grand Slam had been landed.

Between the World Wars, Welsh rugby was unable to repeat its big successes in the years leading up to the First World War. The Great Depression hit hard in the South Wales coal fields, the breeding ground for so much Welsh rugby talent – many of the country's finest players were forced to head to the north of England and earn a wage playing rugby league. The country enjoyed a shared Five Nations title in 1920 with England and Scotland, and then won it outright in 1922, 1931 and 1936. But a second Triple Crown or Grand Slam remained elusive.

Wales captain T Parker tosses up with LG Brown of England before the 1922 game at Cardiff, which Wales won 28-6

Playing mind games

Gareth Edwards listened with a straight face as Welsh team coach John Dawes outlined his plan to introduce codewords at a training session before a match against England. "When you want the left-side flanker to make a break, the codeword should start with a P," said Dawes. "If you want a break on the right side, use a codeword beginning with S." He tossed the ball to master scrum half Edwards, who put it into the scrum and shouted: "Psychology!"

Ireland finished their rough, tough match against Wales at Lansdowne Road in 1882 with just 11 men. Two were carried off and two others walked off in protest at debatable decisions made by the referee Richard Mullock, who also happened to be the secretary of the Welsh Rugby Union.

Wales stride on to the pitch at Cardiff Arms Park for the Five Nations game against England in 1922. They won 28-6

The Welsh team in January 1922 – back row (left to right): touch judge, D Hiddlestone, Rev J G Stephens, T Roberts, S Morris, J Whitfield, W Cummins, referee; middle row: C Richards, J Rees, B Evans, T Parker (capt), T Jones, I Evans, F Palmer; front row: W Bowen, W J Delahay

A Team of Lions

Wales had waited 39 years for a second Grand Slam. The star-studded side of inspirational captain John Gwilliam delivered it in a style which was to herald a triumphant decade

How good were the Wales team of 1950? Perhaps a useful marker of their talent is that 14 of the players who represented Wales in that year's Five Nations travelled with the British Lions in the summer.

The campaign opened against England at Twickenham, and the game was the international debut of an 18-year-old threequarter called Lewis Jones. He produced an astonishing display from full back, capped by a run from inside his own half which took him through England's midfield and set up a fine try for Cliff Davies. Jones also kicked a conversion and a penalty goal as Wales triumphed 11-5.

Next up at Swansea came Scotland, who had already beaten France 8-5 at Murrayfield. The Welsh pack took the sting out of the Scots in the first half and then the home side reverted to a more expansive game that saw the backs take the upper hand and Wales run out 12-0 winners. The third game of the season, against Ireland, proved to be the toughest. The Irish had won the Triple Crown the previous season but faltered in 1950, drawing against France and losing to England before thrashing Scotland 21-0.

The mighty Welsh forwards had dominated their team's opening two games, but they met their match in the Irish pack – and the match became one of grinding attrition.

There was no score in the first 40 minutes but Wales took the lead seven minutes into the second half. Jack Matthews pounced on a loose ball and set Ken Jones away down the left wing to sprint in for a try. Almost immediately, the Irish kicked a penalty to bring the scores level. The mutual forward battering continued throughout the half until, with just three minutes left, Irish fly half Jack Kyle got caught in possession and the ball was fed, via Lewis Jones, to Malcolm Thomas on the left wing. Thomas made for the corner and just managed to ground the ball before being bundled off the pitch by the Irish defence. The winning margin of 6-3 was tight, but good enough to secure the Triple Crown, their first for 39 years.

And to the Triple Crown the Welsh added the Grand Slam with a supremely competent display against France at Cardiff Arms Park which finished 21-0.

The all-conquering Wales team of 1950 back row (left to right): I Jones, G D Robbins, Don Hayward, Roy John, R T Evans, Ray Gale, W B Cleaver; front row: Ken Jones, Malcolm Thomas, Lewis Jones, John G William (capt), Jack Matthews, Cliff Davies, Gerwyn William; (on ground) Rex Willis, D M Davies. Opposite: A 1950s cigarette card pose by Carwyn James

WRU

KEY PLAYER 1950

Ken Jones

The 44 caps Ken Jones collected for Wales between 1947 and 1957 stood as a Welsh record until surpassed by Gareth Edwards in 1976.

Yet Jones did not receive his first cap until he was 26, thanks to a career disrupted by the Second World War, without which he would surely have added many more caps to his name.

Jones was the archetypal flying Welsh winger – he won an Olympic silver sprint relay medal in the London Games in 1948 – and on the rugby pitch he was not only extremely quick, but superbly well-balanced.

He played in 40 consecutive Five Nations matches and was a vital component of the Grand Slam sides of both 1950 and 1952, scoring four tries in each season.

With his upright, leggy running style and the ball customarily tucked under one arm, Jones could conjure tries from the faintest of gaps – as many opposing wingers found to their cost.

Morgan's Masterclass

A second Grand Slam in three seasons for the Welsh was just reward
for the sublime skills of fly half Cliff Morgan and wing Ken Jones
but the real golden age was still to come

Cliff Morgan, opposite,
tries to shrug off Koch of
South Africa during the
British Lions' 1955 tour
which made Morgan
a star on the world stage

After the Grand Slam triumph of 1950, the fact that Wales suffered the following season to finish the Five Nations in third place with just a solitary victory – and a 19-0 drubbing at the hands of Scotland – was a surprise to many. But in the same season, a thrilling battle against South Africa, which was narrowly lost 6-3, showed that the Welsh were made of stern stuff.

The 1952 season started for Wales with what proved to be the clash of that year's titans, v England at Twickenham. In front of 73,000 fans, England, the wooden spoonists the year before, opened up a 6-0 lead thanks to tries by backs AE Agar and JE Woodward, both making their Five Nations debut.

But the Welsh forwards began to claw back possession and territorial superiority. In a thrilling second half, winger Ken Jones scored two superb tries and Malcolm Thomas kicked one vital conversion to secure an 8-6 win.

In the second game of the series Scotland, the team who had humiliated Wales a year before, came to a Cardiff Arms Park packed to the rafters with 56,000 fans.

They witnessed a dour game with little flair or excitement to warm the blood, but the Welsh fans at least went home happy because their team, thanks to another try by Jones and the accurate kicking of Thomas, ran out 11-0 winners. Welsh scrum half Rex Willis was an unsung hero of the game.

He received a blow to the face just before half-time but instead of going off, he played on to the end of the match and only then was it discovered that his jaw was broken in three places.

The Triple Crown, the third for Wales since 1910, was won at Lansdowne Road against Ireland. Jones scored yet another crucial try, at a time when the Welsh were holding on to a narrow lead. Fly half Cliff Morgan broke from inside his own half and Jones came in off the right wing to take a short pass and sprint the length of the Irish half to score. The try put paid to any Irish hopes of revival and Wales triumphed 14-3.

The Welsh claimed their second Grand Slam in three years in front of their own fans at Swansea, but it did not come with a flourish.

The dynamic genius of Morgan at fly half was missing through injury, and the goal-kicking skills of Lewis Jones also took leave of absence for the match as the young centre, playing his final game for Wales before he turned professional and went to rugby league, missed six out of eight attempts at goal.

But the two penalties he did land, along with a drop goal by Alun Thomas, were enough to see Wales home 9-5.

> "Remember his great days:
> as the architect of Wales'
> Triple Crown success at
> Twickenham in 1952;
> as captain in the
> Championship Wales won
> in 1956; as the great
> crowd-puller for Cardiff
> during the whole of
> the '50s; as well as the
> great stand-off for the
> British Isles in South
> Africa in 1955."
>
> GARETH EDWARDS
> on Cliff Morgan in his book
> 100 Great Rugby Players

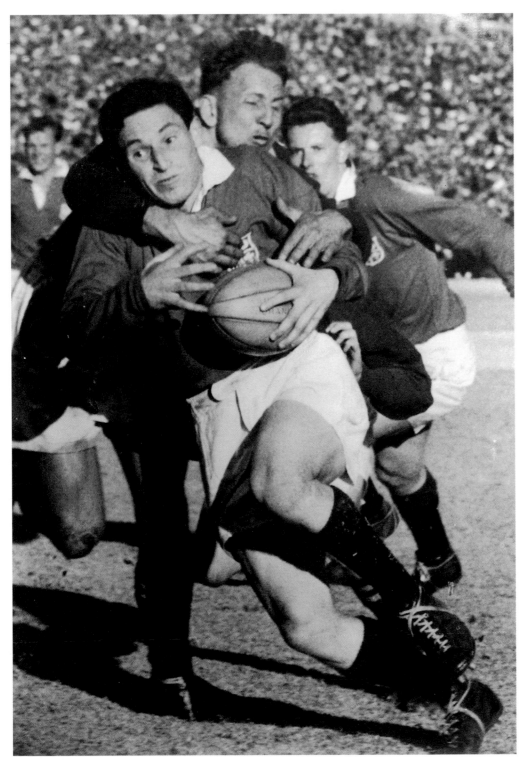

KEY PLAYER 1952

KEY PLAYER 1952

Cliff Morgan

It is a cliché to say that Wales has had a long production line of outstanding players at fly half – but it is also true, and Cliff Morgan stands out as one of the truly great orchestrators of the game wearing (in those days) the No 6 shirt.

Morgan formed the blueprint for a fly half. Sturdy of build at 5ft 7in with bandy legs which supplied an electrifying turn of pace, he had a very safe pair of hands which could ship the ball on at speed, a dazzling body swerve which left opponents floundering and a superb tactical brain.

He made his debut in 1951 and in just his third match for his country he was given a torrid time by the Springboks. But by the 1952 Five Nations, through to his retirement after 29 caps in 1958 (when he was still only 27), he was the preferred choice at the pivotal position for Wales.

Morgan was a powerful draw in rugby, able to light up a game with a moment of brilliance – and the highlight of his career was probably the incomparable performances he gave in South Africa when touring with the 1955 British Lions.

Dragons Breathe Fire

The Welsh are coming. They struggled to swing as the Sixties started
but in the second half of the decade the side was slowly being
built which would light up a generation

Following the Grand Slam of 1952, Wales won outright or shared the Five Nations in 1954, 1955 and 1956, but their fortunes suffered such a downturn as the Swinging Sixties arrived that the Welsh won only one match in the 1962 season and one more in 1963 when they finished the year with the wooden spoon.

The tide began to turn in the 1964 season when Wales, now led by Clive Rowlands, enjoyed their first unbeaten Five Nations for 12 years. Two wins and two draws were good enough to give Wales a share of the championship with Scotland.

1965 – Triple Crown

Rowlands' team went one better in 1965, bringing the Triple Crown back to the valleys, along with the championship.

England were beaten 14-13 at Cardiff Arms Park, and then a powerful Scottish side were narrowly overcome 14-12 at Murrayfield.

Which brought Ireland to Cardiff to contest the Triple Crown and the championship. Demand for tickets to see the match was unprecedented and nigh on 59,000 fans squeezed into a wet and muddy Arms Park to see Ireland control the first 40 minutes. Irish domination, however, was not turned into points and just before the interval, David Watkins snatched an unexpected try for the home side which Terry Price was able to convert.

This took the wind out of Irish sails, and Dewi Bebb stretched the lead with a try from close range after 55 minutes. A monster drop goal by Price, plus a penalty, ensured that victory and the Triple Crown went to Wales,

14-8. The following year, 1966, Wales secured its third Five Nations Championship title in succession, although Ireland thwarted back-to-back Triple Crown ambitions in Dublin by winning 9-6.

1969 – Triple Crown

The Welsh team that started the Five Nations in 1969 contained a host of players who were already, or soon became, giants of the international game. The likes of Gareth Edwards, Barry John and Gerald Davies in the backs were already established in the side, and they were joined at the beginning of the championship by Mervyn Davies at No 8 and JPR Williams at full back. Phil Bennett would make his first appearance in a Welsh jersey later in the campaign.

New Wales coach Clive Rowlands, the former captain, brought a new dimension to the Five Nations build-up for the team by introducing squad training sessions which helped bond the players, particularly the forwards, into a solid unit.

This was a Welsh side capable of playing superb, attacking rugby, reflected in the fact that they scored 14 tries in the campaign, six more than nearest rivals Ireland.

Scotland at Murrayfield was the opening game of the season – and Wales recorded their best start to the championship since 1966 by winning 17-3.

The atmosphere at the home game against Ireland was more muted than normal as Cardiff Arms Park was undergoing reconstruction and capacity was halved to 29,000. What those fans saw was a bad-tempered game which flared up as early as the third minute when

Merve the Swerve, top, and Gerald, of the famous sidestep, two Davieses who inspired Wales

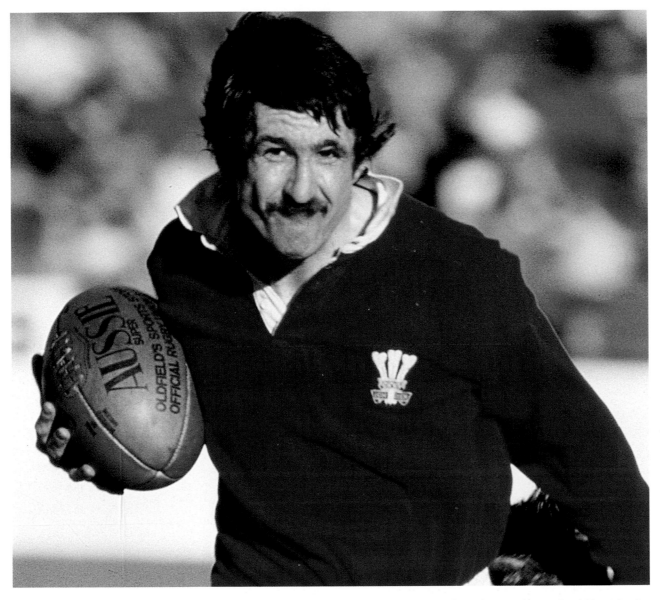

"For half an hour the Irish were absolutely bananas! I was terrified to go down on the ball in case one of them exacted revenge. Phil O'Callaghan, for instance, was frightening just to look at. With his steely eyes and bristling crew cut he reminded you of a villain out of a James Bond film."

GARETH EDWARDS is shaken and stirred after a punch-up with Ireland

Welsh captain Brian Price connected with a haymaker on Ireland's Noel Murphy. Despite the air of mayhem throughout the match, Wales recorded their highest points tally against the Irish since 1920: 24-11, including four tries.

Against France, the Welsh opened up an eight-point lead without reply thanks to a superb try from Gareth Edwards and another by Maurice Richards. The French fought back ferociously to level the scores, and in the end the Welsh were grateful to finish the game 8-8. The Triple Crown was captured in fine style at Cardiff with the dismantling of England 30-9, Wales's biggest margin of victory over the English since 1922. Cardiff winger Maurice Richards was outstanding, scoring four of the team's five tries. Barry John grabbed the other.

This was a Welsh performance in complete contrast to that against Ireland – full of imagination and clean-cut attacking rugby by a team that was clearly destined to go on to even greater things.

WRU

Brilliant Barry

By now the Welsh were unstoppable. England, Scotland and
Ireland all fell to the excellence of Edwards and his partner John.
France, and a first win in Paris for 14 years, proved no problem

The Triple Crowns of the 1960s were turned into Grand Slams in the 1970s as an outstanding Welsh side, inspired by the talents of Gareth Edwards and Barry John, began to show the full flowering of their brilliance. In 1971 they survived an astonishing game against Scotland, winning by a point with a last-gasp John Taylor conversion, to clinch their first Slam for 19 years with their first win in Paris since 1957.

Two more Grand Slams were to come in this decade, in 1976 and '78, and Wales won the championship five more times, never dropping out of the top two.

In 1971 they started their Five Nations season at Cardiff with the visit of an England team fielding seven new caps – and the inexperience showed as the Welsh pack secured complete dominance of the ball, while, behind the scrum, Edwards and John shrewdly controlled the game.

Wales took the lead through a John drop goal, and though England replied with a try from a lineout to level the scores, it soon became one-way traffic. Gerald Davies,

> "All's well that ends well, but when John's kick went over I must have the most relieved Welshman in Edinburgh. I knew only too well that I had handed Scotland two of their penalties on a plate..."
> MERVYN DAVIES
> talks of his relief after the match

Gareth Edwards and
Barry John, opposite,
were major factors in
Wales' domination of
the Five Nations
Championship

Legendary, and that
was just the sideburns.
JPR Williams was one of
the finest players Wales
ever had

Holmes, sweet Holmes

Cardiff and Wales scrum half Terry Holmes was renowned for his fearlessness and power. At his peak he inspired great expectations, and many a story. Wales were playing England at Twickenham and it was a complete sell-out. Taff from Cardiff couldn't get a ticket but was close enough to the back of the terracing to receive a running match commentary from his pal Dai. "Fourteen Welsh players have gone off injured," shouted Dai. "There's only our Terry left against the full England team." Suddenly the crowd let out a mighty roar. "What's happened?" shouted Taff. "Terry's scored, 'as he?"

Team-mates Howie Jones and Harry Peacock dived on the ball simultaneously after chasing it across the line for Wales against Ireland at Swansea in 1930. For the first and only time in international rugby a try was awarded jointly. Wales won 12-7.

"It was a truly wonderful feeling to reach the end of the 1971 Five Nations campaign as both champions and Grand Slam winners for the first time since 1952. I played in two more Grand Slam seasons, in 1976 and 1978, but that first one stands out in my memory, for so many of us were starry-eyed and in our rugby infancy."
GARETH EDWARDS
on the joy of winning in 1971

---

now playing on the wing, scored a brace of tries, and John Bevan, on the other wing, touched down for a try on his debut.

Wales led 16-3 by half-time. There were no further tries in the second half but a penalty by JPR Williams and another John drop goal sealed the game 22-6.

Wales against Scotland at Murrayfield was a different matter altogether, a titanic battle sealed in the end by John Taylor's nerveless kicking skills. It was nip and tuck all the way through – Wales at one point early in the second half led 11-6 but they were pegged back by a Sandy Carmichael try and a third Peter Brown penalty.

John sidestepped and swerved his way over for a try but another penalty by Brown and a try by Chris Rea gave Scotland a four-point lead. With time running out, Edwards unleashed the back line again and Gerald Davies scored 15 yards in from the corner flag.

Most of the Welsh team could not bear to watch as Taylor stepped forward to take the conversion which, if successful, would put Wales into a one-point lead. He calmly stroked the ball between the posts for a 19-18 victory.

The Welsh bandwagon rolled on back in Cardiff where the Triple Crown was won with a 23-9 victory over the Irish, although the margin only became comfortable deep into the second half.

Edwards and John were in awesome form, accounting for 17 of Wales's 23 points. The British Lions squad announced soon after the game contained 11 of the Welsh players on the field that day and they were to play a key role in securing a brave and memorable 2-1 series win over New Zealand.

That left the French. They were no pushovers, having shared the championship with

Barry John

You can't talk of the greatness of Barry John at fly half without referring to the brilliance of his half-back partner, Gareth Edwards. The pair represented Wales together 18 times in the Five Nations and their understanding of each other's game verged on the telepathic.

When John and Edwards met for practice before their first international together in 1967 it was a cold, wet day in Carmarthen. John was not keen on the session and said: "Look, Gareth, you throw them, I'll catch them. Let's leave it at that and go home." Edwards replied: "Don't worry about my passes, I can get them to you from anywhere. Just make sure you catch them." From such a start grew one of the world's most thrilling pairings.

John was an instinctive, sometimes unorthodox player, with an array of skills that set him apart. A fine kicker from the hand and also at goal, John's biggest attribute was his elusive running. Some say he retired too early when he stepped down in 1972 at 27, but his name is etched in international rugby history.

Wales the year before, and their attacking play was at times brilliant. The Welsh, trailing 5-0, replied in kind.

JPR broke away with an interception and ran 70 yards before feeding Edwards, whose try reduced the deficit to two points. Early in the second half a now bloodied John kicked a penalty to put his side into the lead at 6-5.

Then Wales took a scrum against the head, giving John the chance to break the defence and touch down for the score which equalled Keith Jarrett's 31-point championship record and claimed the Grand Slam.

Slamming Dawes

Another Grand Slam in 1976 was the catalyst for a period of extraordinary dominance by the red dragon. Triple Crowns were collected by the handful and glory was never far away

Wales were in their pomp at the end of the 1970s. After a shared second place in the Five Nations in 1974, they won the championship the next season and by 1976, under the guidance of a new captain, No 8 Mervyn Davies, and coach John Dawes, the Grand Slam was soon gloriously collected. It presaged an extraordinary run for Welsh rugby up to 1979, when they secured two Grand Slams and four consecutive Triple Crowns. In 1975 Wales had given notice that something special was on the horizon when they racked up a total of

Steve Fenwick scored 139 points for Wales in the Five Nations

87 points in the campaign, just one fewer than the nation's most prolific year in 1910, and only a narrow 12-10 defeat in Scotland prevented them from landing another Triple Crown and Grand Slam.

However, the spoils were secured in 1976, and in superb fashion. Wales were unbeatable in the midfield, thriving on good possession from the pack, Gareth Edwards and Phil Bennett pulled the strings at half back, and full back JPR Williams proved time and again his brilliance in both attack and defence.

Bennett was in his element in 1976, and through the four matches he notched 38 points, equalling the individual record for a Five Nations series, as Wales easily surpassed their previous best haul with 102.

The season began at Twickenham, and the Welsh put down a strong statement of intent for the year by racking up their record points tally at the ground with a 21-9 victory over England. Edwards scored the first of Wales's three tries and then JPR claimed the other two, the second from a glorious scissors move with fly half Phil Bennett.

There was an element of revenge in the air for the second game of Wales's season because Scotland had robbed the Welsh of the opportunity of the Grand Slam the previous year.

> **"As memorable to me as my two tries in this game was an early tackle on Hignell which stopped him crossing for an opening score. He had support on each side, but tried to run through me. I didn't believe in allowing opponents to do that."**
>
> JPR WILLIAMS
> after victory over England

Twelve months on and the Scots never stood a chance at Cardiff Arms Park.

The match was by no means a classic, but Bennett proved more than effective with his goal-kicking and Edwards notched his 17th try for Wales, equalling the country's all-time record as the Scots were sent packing 28-6. The Triple Crown was secured in Dublin, thanks principally to a devastating second-half spell which sank the Irish at a time when they may have harboured hopes of nullifying the Welsh lead of 16-9.

Bennett enjoyed one of his best attacking games in a Welsh jersey and featured in three of Wales's four tries. By full-time the points gap had widened to 34-9.

And so France came to Cardiff with Wales fully expected to land a fifth Grand Slam and their second in six years.

Landed it was, but the French put up the toughest opposition seen by Wales in the campaign, relying on a strong forward display and a disciplined performance by the half backs which concentrated more on territorial gain than flair. Towards the end of the match the Welsh were holding on as their opponents pounded their line, but, with JPR's defensive resolve again coming to the fore, they held on.

France actually outscored the Welsh by two tries to one, but successful penalties from Bennett (2), Steve Fenwick (2) and another by Allan Martin, an extraordinary effort from 50 yards in the first half, saw Wales through 19-13.

It turned out to be the last game for captain Mervyn "the Swerve" Davies – just weeks later a brain haemorrhage forced his retirement from the game.

The London Welsh and Swansea back-row forward was capped 38 times for Wales and led his country on nine occasions, winning eight of them.

KEY PLAYER 1976

Gareth Edwards

Gareth Edwards is a rugby god in Wales, and revered the world over for his contribution to international rugby with his country, for whom he was capped 53 times at scrum half, and with the British Lions, for whom he played in 10 Test matches.

Edwards may have been fortunate to work with two of the best exponents of the fly half position the world has ever seen – Barry John and Phil Bennett – but the lucky ones were the Welsh fans, the Cardiff star was real dynamite. He was the complete scrum half: a good passer, a bulldozer off the back of the scrum or breakdown, and fast to crop up in support in a try-scoring situation.

For the record Edwards won three Grand Slams, five Triple Crowns and five outright Five Nations titles with his country. Welsh No 9s since have had a hard job to live up to his lofty standards.

Last Action Heroes

Bennett and Edwards retired in 1978, but not before another triumph had been secured, appropriately with two tries by the master fly half to secure his place in Welsh rugby history

Wales followed up their 1976 Grand Slam season with further Five Nations success, although they immediately set a record only partially to be welcomed. In 1977 the Welsh won the Triple Crown but became the first country to do so and still finish second in the Five Nations table, thanks to a 16-9 defeat at the hands of the Grand Slam-winning French.

Wales aimed to go one better in 1978, and the season was one of two powerful sides taking control of the championship with a winner-takes-all face-off on the last weekend of the campaign. France, the champions, and the Welsh won each of their first three games to set up the clash of the titans at Cardiff Arms Park.

Wales's season started at Twickenham, and although they notched their fourth win in five visits to England's HQ, it was not a pretty game. A wet and dismal ground greeted the sides, not the best setting for Gareth Edwards to make his 50th appearance in a Welsh jersey. Neither side succeeded in crossing the try line and it was a tale of kickers – Alistair Hignell kicked two penalties for the

Steve Fenwick had a mighty boot, but was also a devastating runner – though he could not match Old Twinkletoes JPR Williams, opposite

Ray Gravell scored his first international try to help Wales to their 1978 Grand Slam, as Phil Bennett, opposite, bowed out of international rugby on a high

English, but Phil Bennett replied with three for Wales to make the final score 9-6.

The fans who travelled to Cardiff to see Wales's next game, against Scotland, were greeted by bitterly cold conditions. Indeed not long after full-time, the snow fell so heavily that many Scots fans were unable to make the journey home.

But this was a much better game for the spectators. Scotland took the lead with a penalty, while Wales hit back through Gareth Edwards's 20th try for his country. When Jim Renwick then went over the line for Scotland, it looked possible that an upset might be on the cards. Just prior to half-time, though, the Welsh upped their game. Ray Gravell scored his first international try, Bennett dropped a goal and Steve Fenwick and Derek Quinnell added further tries. Phil Bennett slotted a penalty to complete a devastating 20-minute burst. Wales did not press home the advantage further, but enough had been done to keep the Scots at bay, and the final score of 22-14 meant a Triple Crown was the next item on the agenda.

The game at Lansdowne Road was a tough struggle, with the Welsh on the receiving end of a battering from the Irish forwards that frequently skirted the line between the legal and the ferocious. Wales led 13-6 at half-time, but the Irish were at their most physical through the second half and drew level. However, they ran out of steam, and JPR Williams was able to score a vital try to re-establish a lead which would not be overhauled. The Triple Crown was won 20-16.

The French travelled to Cardiff for the Grand Slam decider – a game which also turned out to be the last in a red jersey for both Gareth Edwards and Phil Bennett.

The latter played a vital role in the victory, scoring two tries, the first time a Welsh fly half had done so in a game since 1931, and thanks to seven missed French kicks at goal, Wales ran out 16-7 winners to secure a suitable triumph for their two departing heroes.

KEY PLAYER 1978
Phil Bennett

Phil Bennett had big boots to fill when he first stepped into the Welsh team after the retirement of Barry John in 1972. John had taken the position of fly half for Wales beyond the legendary heights reached by Cliff Morgan before him. Bennett arguably carried the legend even further.

In his early days Bennett was a superb tactical kicker, but did not seem to have the spark to set his threequarters free in the same way that Morgan and John both could. As a result he struggled to hold a regular place in the Welsh team until the 1976 season when he began to play like a changed man.

Always in possession of a superb side-step, the new Bennett added dynamic running to his portfolio and took Wales to great heights, culminating in his captaining of the 1978 Grand Slam-winning team at Cardiff in his last international, his eighth in charge of the side. The 10 points Bennett registered in his final game set a new European record for points in internationals of 166, but there was much, much more to the talents of Phil Bennett than bare statistics can show.

"Although I did not finalise the decision to leave international rugby until later in the year, looking back I am glad to have contributed two tries in my last game for Wales. That seemed a good way of saying thank you for 29 caps and a whole lot of fun."

PHIL BENNETT
on his international retirement

The Long Wait

Wales finished the 1970s in style with a fourth successive Triple Crown
and a 21st Five Nations title. Few would have thought then that
the nation would have to wait nine years for another hint of glory

O n March 17, 1979, full back JPR Williams
announced his retirement from international
rugby after leading his country to a 27-3 drubbing
of England which secured the Welsh a fourth Triple Crown
on the trot, and a 21st outright win of the Five Nations
Championship.

Wales had begun the 1979 season with a Derek
Quinnell-inspired 19-13 victory against the Scots at
Murrayfield, the Welsh No 8 guiding his forwards to a
stranglehold over their opponents.

A hard-earned win over Ireland at Cardiff, 24-21, set
thoughts turning to another possible Grand Slam season,
but those hopes were dashed in Paris by a single point. Still,
victory over England in front of a home crowd secured two
of three potential titles for the season.

After being spoilt with success through the 1960s and
'70s, those fans who watched Wales at Cardiff on the day
JPR retired must have found the disappointment of failure
for the next eight seasons very hard to bear. The Five
Nations title, and the Triple Crown with it, did not return
to Wales until 1988.

1988

In the inaugural World Cup in 1987, Wales had shown
signs of a return to form by advancing all the way to the
semi-finals before being trounced by the All Blacks.
Even then they narrowly beat Australia to win the third
place play-off.

So when the 1988 Five Nations season kicked off for
Wales at Twickenham, there was some reason to suggest the
English could be toppled. And so it proved, 11-3, with

Derek Quinnell, top, was
a storming No 8 and
formidable captain.
Paul Thorburn, right,
turned many matches
with his boot

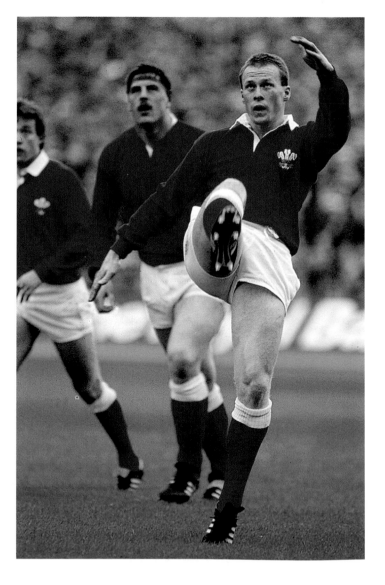

Two classic scores from Welsh heroes: Jonathan Davies, left, outpaces Scotland's Derek White, while below Ieuan Evans touches down after his flight of fancy in the same match

fly half Jonathan Davies leading the way. The next game, against Scotland at Cardiff Arms Park, was a classic, a match that could have been won by either side as the momentum swung back and forth.

Davies again was influential, opening the scoring with a breathtaking turn of pace to collect his own kick ahead after outpacing the Scottish forwards. Then winger Ieuan Evans danced his way to an extraordinary try, sidestepping past most of Scotland's defence to score under the posts.

The Scots fought back with their own well-worked tries, but Wales triumphed 25-20 to set up the chance of the Triple Crown in the next game in Dublin.

The match against the Irish was not one to stay in the memory, the home side working hard to spoil Welsh opportunities despite their superiority. But full back Paul Thorburn's rock-steady play and accurate goal-kicking

secured the Triple Crown 12-9. Wales were unable to go one step further and emulate the Grand Slam of 1978, falling to France in Cardiff 10-9 having squandered several chances. But the Triple Crown and a share of the championship at least brought success back to the valleys.

"I'm not the emotional type but I don't mind admitting I do become quite emotional about that. Whenever I feel low, I watch it on video and suddenly I feel a lot better. I get a tremendous buzz when I see it, or when someone says it was the best try he, or she, had seen."

IEUAN EVANS
on his brilliant try against Scotland

A Ray of Light

One championship in the 1980s was matched by a sole triumph in the '90s as Welsh fans were forced to make the most of their team's rare victories. The consolation came when the title was paraded at Twickenham

There were few indications that the Welsh would enjoy a winning season in 1994. They had ended the previous Five Nations rock bottom and then lost at home to Canada. But that result, though a shoddy performance, turned out to be a blip. For the Five Nations the Welsh were flat out for success – starting with the Scots visiting Cardiff Arms Park in a downpour.

A tough display up front led to good Welsh possession for the backs, and replacement winger Mike Rayer made the most of it, splashing through the puddles for two superb tries in a 29-6 win.

In the second game of the series, against Ireland in Dublin, the Welsh, with Neil Jenkins scoring all their points, played a tight, controlled game which, despite the narrow 17-15 score, they were never in danger of losing.

For the match against France in Cardiff, No 8 Scott Quinnell, son of 1978 Grand Slammer Derek, was the driving force of a fantastic Welsh win over a powerful visiting side. Quinnell was rampant, scoring one try and setting up winger Nigel Walker for another. France, the champions of 1993, were comprehensively beaten 24-15.

So a Grand Slam possibility emerged if England could be beaten at Twickenham. Unfortunately the Welsh were unable to raise their game to the heights they had enjoyed in their previous matches. England were too good, but Wales did at least win the championship, their only success in the 1990s.

Outstanding displays by Scott Quinnell, son of Derek, and Mike Rayer, far right, helped Wales to the championship in 1994, allowing a delighted captain Ieuan Evans to collect the trophy at a dismayed Twickenham

Scotland

Perennial underdogs, Scotland have thrived on defying expectations, and the English in particular. While they cannot boast the best record in the championship, there could hardly be more popular winners of the last ever Five Nations

Flowering Scotland – lock Scott Murray and No 8 Stuart Reid hold the line during their triumph in the last Five Nations Championship

BY
GAVIN HASTINGS

'from that day, I was hooked on the five Nations'

Gavin Hastings scored more points in the Five Nations Championship than any other player. Scotland's top scorer in all Tests, and third in the history of world rugby, he was an unerring kicker and a courageous full-back, the rock on which the Scots built their team for 10 years. Gavin played for Scotland 61 times, captaining his country on 20 occasions, and was a driving force in the team that won the 1990 Grand Slam. The only Scot who has won more caps is his brother – and, as Gavin testifies here, the Five Nations was in their blood from an early age...

My first experience of the Five Nations was in 1971 when my dad took me along to Murrayfield to see Scotland play Wales. There I was, nine years of age, sitting in the West Stand in the middle of this huge, huge crowd, facing the massive East Terrace and the thousands and thousands of Welsh supporters who had made the pilgrimage up to Scotland. It was a wonderful atmosphere and very exciting for a young boy.

It was a cracking game of rugby, too, end-to-end stuff, and I can remember the crucial incidents even now. Halfway through the second half Chris Rea scored a try for Scotland right in front of the posts. I watched Peter Brown clatter an easy conversion kick off the right-hand post, and I thought, 'Oh dear, that could cost Scotland' – and so it proved. Right at the death Gerald Davies scored a try, and John Taylor took the goal from out on the right-hand side with his left foot and drilled it between the posts to give

Wales victory by one point. Taylor was a flanker in those days, so you had a No 8 taking the conversions and penalties for Scotland, and a flanker kicking goals for Wales.

My memory of John Taylor is very clear: his hair all over the place and a bushy beard, a really raggedy-taggedy sort of Welshman (he won't thank me for that!). His conversion made it 19-18 and Wales went on to win the Grand Slam. Even as a nine-year-old, I could tell it was a classic game. From that day, I was hooked on the Five Nations.

Two years later, I saw Scotland get their revenge against the Welsh with a one-point victory of their own. But perhaps the most memorable match I ever attended at Murrayfield was the 1975 Scotland-Wales Five Nations game, played out in front of a world record crowd of 104,000. I remember sitting in the schoolboy enclosure – in those days they had four or five rows in front of the terracing all the way round. People were spilling over into the enclosure and we eventually had to move from our seats

The order of the boot –
Hastings' commanding
kicking usually gave
Scotland the edge

and go to sit in front of the advertising hoardings, simply because there were so many spectators there. It was an amazing atmosphere, and Scotland came away the winners in another tight contest, 12-10.

As kids, the big highlight was every two years when the Welsh came. Once, when we were about 15, we nicked a leek off the Welsh, a huge thing about 15 feet tall made from a drainpipe. We used to take it to all the games – it didn't matter whether we were playing England, France or Ireland – and meet underneath it on the East Terrace. Someone would just plonk this leek down under that wonderful big scoreboard and we'd all gather round. To my mind those were magic days, everyone piling in together.

My first game for Scotland was in the Five Nations in 1986, and what an occasion it was. My brother Scott and I had both played in the trial for the Possibles against the Probables, and we had thumped them by about 42-15, so we had high hopes of getting the call-up. I was home from Cambridge for my Christmas holidays when the team was announced, and I was still asleep when the envelope arrived in the post. Scott came into my room, woke me up and said, "Well, I'm in," and then buggered off to work without bothering to find out whether I had made the team or not. Typical Scott. That night, we celebrated in the good old-fashioned style, drinking champagne and beer and anything else that was put in front of us until two in the morning. In

those days the Scotland team didn't meet until two days before the match. We had a training session the previous Sunday and then again on the Thursday and a quick runaround on Friday, and that was the preparation for a Five Nations match! Today's players wouldn't believe it.

There were six new caps in the Scotland team to play France that day, including David Sole, Finlay Calder, Matt Duncan and Jeremy Campbell-Lamerton, the son of Mike, who captained the Lions. Everyone had written us off, saying there was no way that a Scotland team with six new caps could possibly upset the French, but that's exactly what we did do. We got stuck into them and we continued to do that throughout most of my career in the matches at Murrayfield.

Yet again it was a one-point margin of victory. We beat them 18-17 and I kicked a record six penalties – though I think that if I'd kicked even half-decently I would probably have had nine or ten. People often ask me what was my most difficult kick in international rugby, and I always say it was the first, because you've never been in that situation before. I was incredibly nervous, but I just thought, 'Whatever you do, keep your head down.' I managed to do that and thankfully the ball went between the sticks. What a game. To get one's international career off to that sort of start, at home, in the Five Nations, was just incredible. It was a memorable night as well!

Perhaps, though, the best Five Nations game I ever played in was probably later that same season. We beat England 33-6 at Murrayfield, and I kicked eight out of eight. It's almost unimaginable now that you could beat England by that many points. We only beat the Auld Enemy twice in my Five Nations career, and the way we put them to the sword that day made it very, very special. We were scoring tries all over the place.

Our other victory over England came in 1990, of course, when we won 13-7 at Murrayfield. With both teams vying for the Grand Slam, it was an incredibly tense match. England, to be fair, had played brilliant rugby in the lead-up to the game, yet I honestly never doubted that we

"Winning the 1990 Grand Slam was brilliant, yet I think what the players achieved in 1999, and the manner in which they did it, was the equal of that."

GAVIN HASTINGS
salutes his successors

There was no Gavin Hastings to inspire from full back in 1999 but captain Gary Armstrong, far right, was still left holding the trophy at the end of the tournament

would win. To clinch the Grand Slam was brilliant – it's something tangible no one can ever take away from you.

Yet I think what the players achieved in the 1999 championship, and the manner in which they did it, was certainly the equal of that. The 1984 Grand Slam was unique because it hadn't been achieved for almost 60 years, and 1990 was incredible, too. But to my mind, 1999 ranks alongside them. It never fails to amaze me how people continue to write Scotland off.

They simply don't understand the Scottish psyche or appreciate that we're actually quite a proud nation. Winning the final Five Nations was more than just luck. All the guys needed was a good start against Wales, and all of a sudden they were up and running and getting

better with every game. What pleased me most was that it was a team triumph. There's no question Gary Armstrong, Gregor Townsend and John Leslie were instrumental in the adventurous way the backs played – they were all brilliant. But equally important were the forwards, folk like Gordon Bulloch, Scott Murray, Stuart Grimes, Eric Peters, Martin Leslie, Budge Pountney, Peter Walton. They delivered to their ability in a team environment and that was impressive.

Of course, what makes it even sweeter for us Scots is that it was England who were ousted from the winners' podium by Scott Gibbs's injury-time try at Wembley. We opened the '90s with a championship and closed the '90s with a championship, but in between we've not had an awful lot of change out of England. I think, to be fair, that they have had a wee bit of luck against Scotland – such as Jon Callard's last-minute penalty to win the match in 1994 – and I just believe this year Scotland had the better luck.

So Scotland are the last ever holders of the Five Nations Championship, and even an Englishman would have to agree that their victory was good for the tournament.

The '90s were the decade of the Grand Slam – three for England, two for France and one for Scotland – and if England had done it again, some people might have been inclined to dismiss the Five Nations as uncompetitive.

But this year's championship was the equal of any southern hemisphere tournament. The Tri-Nations doesn't have the history, it doesn't have the tradition, it doesn't have the number of teams. The Five Nations is unique and it couldn't have ended on a better note. If someone had written a drama like that, you'd think it could never happen. Well, it happened and it was great.

So next year Italy join and it's the Six Nations, and I just hope they can be competitive. The Five Nations was a unique tournament. It gave people a reason for living in the winter – those memorable weekends in Edinburgh and Dublin and Cardiff and Paris (and we'd better mention Twickenham, or the English will be upset). A Six Nations trip to Rome will be very appealing as well, and we look forward to welcoming Italy. But there's no doubt the Five Nations has been a magnificent tournament and let's hope the Six Nations continues in the same vein.

GAVIN HASTINGS' ALL-TIME SCOTLAND FIVE NATIONS XV

Gavin Hastings would probably be the first name on anyone else's All-Time Scotland team sheet, so you can't blame him for wanting to play in his Five Nations dream team himself. Gavin's XV is based mostly on the two Grand Slam sides of 1984 and 1990, and includes a large number of players he played alongside for Scotland. "I certainly wouldn't mind playing in that line-up," he said. "It's a pretty formidable team."

1 David Sole (Loosehead prop)
The ultimate competitor and a brilliant player with a very good rugby brain. A very hard man, fiercely determined, he was a true winner whichever team he played for.

2 Colin Deans (Hooker) Captain
A wee pocket battleship of a player who I would probably have as captain. He was the first Scotland skipper I played under, and he was a very inspirational player. He wore his heart on his sleeve and led from the front, right in the middle of the front row.

3 Ian Milne (Tighthead prop)
It's very important to have someone who can shore up the scrum, and no one I played with was better at that than Ian. His natural strength was just unbelievable. If you want the ultimate team, you must have the ultimate scrummager. Ian Milne was that man.

4 Chris Gray (Lock)
This one will surprise a few people: Chris Gray at No 2 in the lineout. Chris was very underrated. He played extremely well for Scotland both in

the 1990 Grand Slam and when we went on tour that year to New Zealand. He was a genuine grafter in the lineout and in open play, and his scrummaging was very strong as well. He didn't specialise in the glamour roles but was a real team player.

5 Scott Murray (Lock)
This guy has been outstanding for Scotland in his first year of Five Nations rugby. He totally dominated the lineout against England. He's a real athlete with a hard edge to his play, and he will be an outstanding lock forward in the modern era. I wouldn't be surprised to see him on future Lions tours. He's a tremendous young player who potentially has as much talent as All Black Ian Jones, if not more. That's quite a compliment.

6 John Jeffrey (Blindside flanker)
John was tremendously effective. He was in the thick of everything, extremely competitive, a real rugged farmer. Not only was John a great guy on the field, he was great off it as well, very good for team spirit. He was a perfect foil to Finlay Calder.

7 Finlay Calder (Openside flanker)
A great rugby player, tremendous with the ball in hand going forward and a good bloke to have in your team. He was a hard, hard man and very competitive. I played many years with him, and always admired the way he conducted himself. Finlay had all the qualities you look for in a rugby player.

8 John Beattie (No 8)
A swashbuckling player who made a big impact when he came on the scene in 1980, and on the '83 Lions tour to New Zealand. John was a great athlete and a different kind of No 8, very quick with good hands. I played with him in 1986 against England, when we beat them 33-6 at Murrayfield, and he was everywhere.

9 Gary Armstrong (Scrum half)
In the '99 championship Gary showed all his best qualities. He is the most competitive player I've ever seen on the field; only South Africa's Joost van der Westhuizen comes close. Gary's enthusiasm for the game is unbelievable, and his terrier-like qualities make him an absolute menace to the

Gavin would be more than happy to let Colin Deans, opposite top, captain his dream team, as long as he could be in it, too, alongside his great friend John Jeffrey

opposition. He has been around for 11 seasons of international rugby and has had his fair share of injuries as well, but his professionalism has helped him to continue playing a lot longer than he might otherwise have done.

10 John Rutherford (Outside half)

John was a brilliant stand-off. Towards the end of his career he could really do everything. He could beat a man, he could kick brilliantly, he could read a game, he was a lovely passer of the ball. He was a good defensive player, too, and I would have no hesitation in putting him in the stand-off hot seat.

11 Iwan Tukalo (Left wing)

I played a lot with Iwan and always enjoyed his company. A natural left wing who would always come in off his left foot, he gave the team another dimension. Again, a very competitive player. He certainly knew where the try line was and scored a good few tries for Scotland in his time.

12 Jim Renwick (Inside centre)

Jim was a real playmaker. I remember him playing magnificently when Scotland beat Wales 34-18 at Cardiff in '82, after they hadn't won there for 20 years. He was jinky, he was elusive, he had a wonderful pass, and he was strong in the tackle. I never played with him at international level, but Jim would be great to have in your team.

13 Scott Hastings (Outside centre)

You probably won't be surprised to read this, but I'll run my brother Scott at outside centre. He is Scotland's most-capped player, with 65 appearances, yet he tends to be underrated. Scott was probably known more for his defensive qualities than his attacking prowess. With all these guys around him, he would be a crucial team player. I think we've played together more than 50 times for Scotland, which means I know his game pretty well.

14 Andy Irvine (Right wing)

Andy goes on the wing – and not only because I want to accommodate myself at full back. After all, he played on the right wing for the Lions when J P R Williams was full back, and he thrived there thanks to his pace and knack of being in the right place at the right time. Andy Irvine was an extremely talented player and a bit of an enigma in his time. And, with all due respect to all the other right wingers who have played for Scotland, I can't think of a better man to have on the wing in my ultimate Scottish team.

15 Gavin Hastings (Full back)

I would have to have myself at full back, simply because I really want to play in that team. It's not arrogance: I don't want to come across as though I would have been selected by anyone else. But if it's my Five Nations team, I want to play in it. As for kicking, I would say Andy should take that job. Then I don't have the hassle, and I can just enjoy playing in this fantastic team.

16 Gregor Townsend (Substitute)

Gregor deserves a mention after his season in the '99 Five Nations: he has been a magician. He's unlucky not to be in, so he'd be first reserve, covering centre and stand-off. His feat of scoring a try against each nation in the same season is a superb achievement.

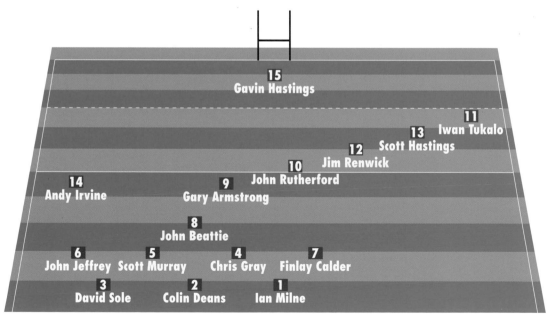

The Roaring Twenties

Scottish fans were made to wait for success after France made it the
Five Nations Championship early this century. But when the triumph came,
the Flying Scotsman, Ian Smith, ensured it was sealed with a flourish

....

Scotland had barely figured as a force in the Five Nations since its inception in 1910. Indeed, they had to look back to 1907, three years before the addition of France to the championship, for a taste of success when they beat each of the other Home nations.

But promising signs emerged in the 1920s, three wins in the 1923 season and then again in 1924 elevating the Scots to second. The 1925 season was to promise even more.

It began at the Inverleith ground in Edinburgh, but would finish at the brand new Scottish headquarters built at Murrayfield. France were the last country to visit Inverleith, and they were met by a dominant Scottish performance. The Scots ran in seven tries, something they had only achieved once before, back in 1910, again against the French. Ian Smith was the main destroyer this time, the winger, part of an all-Oxford University threequarter line, helping himself to four tries in a 25-4 rout.

Six more tries followed for Scotland at Swansea as the Welsh were put to the sword 24-14. Smith again scored four times and his total of eight tries in the season – he was unable to touch down in the next two games – equalled the record of England's prolific Cyril Lowe.

The Irish were overcome at Lansdowne Road 14-8 – Scotland's fourth successive victory over Ireland – and that left England arriving as the first visitors to the new Scottish home of Murrayfield, with the stakes as high as possible. Victory for Scotland would bring the country's sixth Triple Crown, but more importantly, their first Grand Slam. And England came as a formidable force, having recorded 13 games in the championship without defeat, although they had drawn 6-6 with Irish at Twickenham that year.

Nearly 70,000 fans packed into Murrayfield, almost three times the number that had been able to watch at Inverleith, and they cheered their country to the Grand Slam as Scotland won 14-11. Two more Scottish tries in the match, including another for AC Wallace, who scored in each game of the championship, meant the home side established a new Scottish record for the tournament with a total of 17 in the series. The 77 points accumulated in the four matches was also a national record.

It would be a long time before the Scots were again able to toast a Grand Slam, but the 1925 campaign did at least signal the start of a more successful period for Scottish rugby.

"He's only gone and brought lemons" – Scotland's 1927 team against France take a half-time break, below, while the Scots tussle with England in '23, above

Success breeds success

The Grand Slam triumph of 1925 triggered a period of Five Nations success for Scotland which was to last the rest of the decade.

1926 – Joint Champions

Scotland successfully defended their title in 1926, and, with victories against France and Wales, notched six wins in a row in the championship, their best run for 40 years.

The French, destined to remain winless for the third season in a row, were no match for the Scots, only narrowly avoiding their heaviest defeat ever against them when they went down 20-6.

Wales travelled to Murrayfield intent on stifling Scotland's potent back line, and, to an extent, the plan proved a success as they conceded only one try, but that was enough to ensure an 8-5 defeat.

Scotland's winning sequence was brought to a halt by the tournament favourites Ireland at Murrayfield. A tight game was decided by the only score, a try touched down by the Irish winger J H Gage on his debut.

Despite that setback, with Ireland losing 11-8 against Wales the week before, the Scots were still able to clinch a share of the championship by beating England 17-9 in a convincing display at Twickenham.

1927 – Joint Champions

Scotland made it three championships in a row in 1927 – once again sharing the title with the Irish as both secured three wins out of four.

France, still the poor relations of Five Nations rugby (they ended with another wooden spoon in 1927 although a 3-0 victory against England did bring to a halt the country's run of 15

straight defeats), were well beaten at Murrayfield 23-6, with the home side running in four tries.

A fifth consecutive win against Wales then followed as Scotland triumphed 5-0 at the Cardiff Arms Park, but hopes of a Grand Slam were again dashed by the Irish, this time at Lansdowne Road, in appalling weather conditions by 6-0, courtesy of two tries.

A comprehensive victory over England, however, by 21-13 at Murrayfield, ensured at least a share of the championship title. Scotland's points tally included five tries, with two more for the dynamic wing Ian Smith.

1929 – Champions

The Scots' run of success ground to a halt in the 1928 season, a single win and three defeats consigning them to a share of the wooden spoon in the country's worst season since 1911.

In the next campaign Scotland opened against France, who this time showed more resilience, though they were destined to claim the wooden spoon for the sixth time in six years. Scotland ran out 6-3 winners at Murrayfield and the slow start to the season continued with the next game, against the Welsh at Swansea. Wales put an end to a run of four Scottish wins on Welsh soil, and also to any optimism there may have been about the chances of a second Scottish Grand Slam. Four tries in a 14-7 victory meant Scotland had only the championship title to play for.

And that was duly clinched outright, first with a 16-7 victory against Ireland in Dublin in front of 40,000 fans hoping to cheer the Irish to a third successive win of the season. Then more than 80,000 turned up at Murrayfield to see Scotland beat England 12-6 and ensure the they finished the decade on a high.

KEY PLAYER 1925

Ian Smith

Speedy winger Ian Smith, nicknamed rather predictably 'The Flying Scotsman', made a dramatic debut in international rugby, taking to the field in a Scottish shirt for the first time against Wales in 1924, and scoring a hat-trick of tries as Wales were swept aside 35-10.

Smith was particularly devastating in the 1925 Grand Slam season, accumulating eight tries in all, four against Wales and four against France, to tie the championship record of Cyril Lowe.

Smith drifted out of the Scotland side in the late 1920s before making a return, and being appointed captain of the national side in 1933, despite being one of the players remaining from the Scotland side ignominiously whitewashed the previous year. Smith then led Scotland to the Triple Crown.

In all Smith played 32 times for Scotland, 31 of those caps in the Five Nations, the other against South Africa. He scored 24 international tries in his career: nine against England, eight against Wales, six against France, but, curiously, only one against Ireland, despite playing nine times against them.

The Lean Years

Only fleeting glory followed the Grand Slam highs of the 1920s as
Scotland were brought down to earth with a bump and two
Triple Crowns were small consolation for 35 years of frustration

That Scotland, after winning the championship for the fourth time in five years in 1929, then proceeded to finish bottom of the table the following season, was an early indication of hard times ahead.

The years from 1930 to 1964 when the team finally finished top of the table again (albeit sharing the title with Wales) were characterised by some appalling seasons, with few indicators for optimism. Take, for example, the 1950s: Scotland managed to finish with the wooden spoon or a share of it on no fewer then six occasions, including four seasons out of five between 1952 and 1956.

The highlights of these bleak years for Scotland were the two Triple Crown triumphs of 1933 and 1938, during the period when the Five Nations was temporarily reduced to four with France not competing because of an argument over payments to players.

1933 – Champions of the Isles

Scotland reigned supreme in 1933 – a surprise to some as the team had finished bottom the previous season with no wins and a points record of 11 points for in three games, and 42 conceded.

The Scottish restructured for the 1933 season, however, introducing eight new caps for the opening game against Wales, and it became clear that the defence was built on much more solid foundations than had been the case a year previously. Wales were beaten 11-3 at home, a comfortable win which set the Scottish bandwagon rolling.

England then came to Murrayfield and were shut out by an unchanged Scottish side. The 3-0 scoreline in favour of

Scotland reflected a tight affair, but the victory meant that the trip to Ireland, defending champions from 1932, offered the Scots the chance of grabbing both the championship title and the Triple Crown.

Despite conceding two tries, the Scots managed to win by 8-6 thanks to two drop goals. The Triple Crown was justified reward in captain Ian Smith's 32nd and last match for Scotland.

1938 – Champions again

The 1938 season was a high-scoring one, breaking the record for the most points (176) and most tries (35). England ran in 10 touchdowns and scored 60 points in their three games, but still finished only third.

The key game of the series turned out to be the Scots' first match, which was at Murrayfield against Wales, who had already defeated England 14-8 and would end up as runners-up. Scotland won 8-6, but the crucial points came just before the end thanks to a questionable penalty decision which allowed W H Crawford, who scored all his country's points, to slot home the winning kick.

Ireland proved a thorn in Scotland's side during the lean times of the first half of this century and in fact from 1935 to 1954, this was the only year in which the Scots managed victory against them. But it was achieved in style, with four tries in a 23-14 rout.

That left just the Auld Enemy at Twickenham, and they were outclassed 21-16 as Scotland ran in five tries, the most they had scored on England's home turf. It was to be a long time before Scotland tasted such success again.

Wales take on Scotland in 1929, above. Jim Telfer, opposite, can look back on an illustrious playing and coaching career with the Scots

A Crumb of Comfort

Scotland finally broke their miserable run when the Five Nations title
was shared with Wales in 1964 and a certain Jim Telfer, destined for
glory with his country and the Lions, sparkled in his debut season

Scotland took heart from their performance in the 1964 championship. The team won three of their four matches, while Wales scored two wins and two draws, and the Scots were also lifted by a first win in 14 matches against England.

The season started against France, however, at Murrayfield, where a clean sheet was kept in wet conditions, though the 10-0 scoreline may have been flattering to the Scots as the French spurned several good opportunities. Making their first appearances in the Five Nations in a Scottish jersey were three players who went on to become giants in Scottish rugby history: Jim Telfer, Peter Brown and Stewart Wilson.

The Welsh, having drawn 6-6 at Twickenham with England, proved too strong for the Scottish at Cardiff Arms Park, claiming an 11-3 victory.

But winning ways were restored for the Scots at Lansdowne Road three weeks later in a grinding display in which the only points on either side came courtesy of penalty kicks – two by Wilson, Scotland's full back, against the one by his opposite number, Tom Kiernan.

Scotland saved their best performance of the season until last, against England at Murrayfield. For 13 seasons in succession, Scotland had failed to beat the English – home or away.

But three converted tries helped the Scots cruise to a 15-6 victory, a win that was constructed on a platform of forward domination, particularly by Brown in the lineout and Telfer in the back row, with the latter crowning his fine performance by scoring Scotland's third try. The scoreline actually flattered England, as their points tally was boosted only in the last minutes by a pushover try. The win triggered a spell of superiority over the English at Murrayfield where Scotland won five of their next six encounters against the bitterest enemy.

While Scotland were comfortably beating England, however, the Welsh were scrambling their way to the top of the table with an 11-11 draw against the French at Cardiff Arms Park. It came courtesy of a late try by Stuart Watkins which was then converted, denying Scotland the championship outright.

All Tied Up

In the most curious of Five Nations seasons, each team finished the series with two victories after winning their home matches. That meant they all scored four points, and ended in a bizarre five-way tie

Andy Irvine, above, made his Five Nations debut in 1973

An outright title had eluded Scotland since 1938 so a share of the championship in '73 along with the other four nations was little comfort in their centenary year. The only consolation was that the season brought some rousing performances, none more so than in the defeat of the Welsh at Murrayfield.

But the campaign started in France, with the first ever Five Nations game at the new Parc des Princes Stadium in Paris. Unfortunately, the game was not the showpiece many would have liked to open France's new national HQ and the home side had to rely on the boot of debutant Jean-Pierre Romeu, who finished with a 12-point haul, to kick them to a narrow 16-13 victory.

Scotland were led out at Murrayfield for their next match, against a star-studded Welsh side fresh from crushing England 25-9, by a new captain, Ian McLauchlan.

He inspired his team to a fast start and even though Wales could call on the likes of JPR Williams, Gerald Davies, Phil Bennett and Gareth Edwards, the Scots found themselves 10-0 ahead after just 20 minutes, thanks to tries from Colin Telfer and Billy Steele. That Wales clawed it back to 10-9 by the end thanks to three

> "Rugby is a funny game where reputations count for little and all men are equal in the eyes of William Webb Ellis... Over the years, Scotland and Ireland, more than any other countries, have produced some major surprises when least expected, by hustling better sides out of their rhythm to such an extent that they never recover in time to save the match. That crisp February afternoon was just such a day."
> SCOTLAND FULL BACK ANDY IRVINE on victory over Wales

penalty kicks, belied the fact that the Scots were the better team on the day, and the Welsh stars, particularly Edwards at scrum half, were never allowed to flourish.

The momentum of victory against Wales was continued into Scotland's next game at Murrayfield, against the Irish, who had run up five successive wins against the Scots before this encounter.

With the help of three drop goals, two from Dougie Morgan and one from Ian McGeechan, the Irish were beaten 19-14, setting up the prospect of a Triple Crown clash with England at Twickenham.

Hopes were high, but the closest the Scottish got was when they pulled back to 14-13 after Steele scored a try, his second of the match, which was converted by Andy Irvine.

England's forward play was always too strong for the Scots, no doubt partly because the visiting captain McLauchlan was returning to the fray just three weeks after breaking a leg while playing against the Irish.

A number of other Scottish forwards were also carrying injuries, and the final English victory margin of 20-13 comfortably put paid to Scotland's Triple Crown hopes.

Against the Odds

All but written off before the start, Scotland rampaged through the
1984 Five Nations to end 59 years of waiting and claim their second
Grand Slam with a sweet victory over France at Murrayfield

....

The Scottish team which assembled for the 1984 Five Nations Championship should have been paid more respect before the campaign got under way. Eager to end so many years without success, and coached by Jim Telfer, who had shouldered the blame for the British Lions' defeats in New Zealand the previous year, the Scots had warmed up for the tournament with a 25-25 draw against the touring All Blacks at Murrayfield a month before Christmas, a performance to set alarm bells ringing throughout the Home Unions.

The opening match of the campaign for the Scots was a trip to Cardiff to take on the Welsh, who were mindful that Scotland had emerged victorious at the last meeting between the two sides at Cardiff Arms Park.

The Scottish victory, 15-9, came courtesy of strong forward play backed up with good defence and accurate goal-kicking by Peter Dods. The Gala full back, who had made his debut for Scotland the season before, kicked two conversions and a penalty to add to tries by Iain Paxton and captain Jim Aitken.

England's preparations for the Five Nations had included a win over the All Blacks, and the English arrived at Murrayfield for the 100th Calcutta Cup encounter in confident mood. But Scotland had picked out the English full back Dusty Hare for special treatment, and fly half John Rutherford rained down accurate high balls on the No 15, who invariably had a Scottish runner to deal with as well as the ball.

The tactics knocked Hare out of his stride, his place-kicking suffered as a result and he was successful with just two penalty kicks out of eight. The Scots' centre pairing of

The peerless
John Rutherford put
Dusty Hare on the rack

David Johnston and Euan Kennedy both scored tries and Scotland completed stage two of the Grand Slam run with an 18-6 victory.

The next stage was to secure a Triple Crown triumph, the first since 1938, against the Irish in Dublin. Ireland had completed the Triple Crown themselves the previous year, but their team were showing signs of ageing, and were no match for the Scots, who were inspired by Roy Laidlaw. The scrum half scored a brace of tries in a 32-9 romp to set up the Grand Slam decider against the French at Murrayfield. With France also on three victories, whoever won that game would take the great prize.

France took the early lead on that momentous day at the home of Scottish rugby, but when half-time came and

"Captain of the Grand Slam team was Jim Aitken, the Gala prop. Now it's certainly a great honour to captain Scotland at any time but particularly when they win the Slam. But I reckon Aitken was lucky. He was given a team which was exactly the right blend and would have won for anyone."
HOOKER COLIN DEANS
is obviously delighted
for his skipper

That's enough chatter, laddie – Iain Paxton keeps England quiet in the lineout, left, while Peter Dods, right, has plenty to shout about on his way to a record points haul

the Scots trailed only 6-3, Dods having kicked the first of his five penalties in reply to a converted try by French mastermind scrum half Jerome Gallion, the home fans sensed the possibility of victory and the French team became skittish at their inability to dominate the game.

Scotland plugged away, and the French began to give away silly penalties which Dods, on his way to a national record 50 points for the season, gratefully kicked.

Then the real turning point came with 20 minutes remaining. Gallion, the French captain, was stretchered off unconscious after a collision with two opposition forwards, and the Scots took the upper hand. At 12-12 with 10 minutes left, Colin Deans threw into a lineout near the French goal line and the ball, deflected towards the French replacement scrum half Pierre Berbizier, was tantalisingly up for grabs for a split second.

Flanker Jim Calder pounced first to touch down for a try, and the reliable Dods slotted the conversion, as well as another penalty for good measure in the last minute.

The Scottish Grand Slam of 1984 was claimed 21-12, and 59 years of frustration were over.

KEY PLAYER 1984

John Rutherford

Possibly Scotland's most complete fly half in the post-War period, John Rutherford of Selkirk formed a deadly partnership at half back with Roy Laidlaw.

The pair first played in tandem in 1974, for a Borders Under-21 side against a touring Argentina Under-21 team, and the rapport was immediate. For the national side, Rutherford and Laidlaw teamed up 35 times and of the eight games they missed as a partnership, the Scots lost seven.

Rutherford had a superb all-round game, although in his earlier days his kicking was, at best, adequate. However, English full back Dusty Hare, specially treated in 1984, would testify that he soon improved.

But it was the grace and agility of Rutherford's running game which caught the eye. He always seemed to have the time to take the right option and he could make space effortlessly. From his international debut in 1979 to the day when injury at the 1987 World Cup cut short his career, John Rutherford ensured that Scotland would always have the edge at fly half.

Battles of Hastings

Scotland bounced back from a whitewash in 1985 to claim a
share of the championship with France the next season – helped,
for the first of many times, by the debut-making brothers

From the highs of the Grand Slam, to the lows of the wooden spoon. In 1985 Scotland slid straight into the doldrums for the defence of their title won so superbly the year before, with four games and four defeats, although the widest margin was only eight points against France. And the rollercoaster of Scottish rugby continued into the next season, the team bouncing back to record three wins and sneak into a share of the Five Nations Championship with France.

Scotland actually beat France in the campaign, by a single point at Murrayfield, 18-17. Gavin Hastings made his debut for his country and settled into the scoring routine

Making their points –
Gavin Hastings, above,
on his way to a record
against France, Roy
Laidlaw, right, scoring
against Ireland, and
Scott Hastings, far
right, bursting through
the midfield in his
debut season

Colin Deans

The Hawick hooker, first capped in 1978, had already tasted the highs of a Scottish Grand Slam in 1984 by the time of the 1986 season when he was captain of his national team.

A lightweight by modern-day standards at under 13 stones, Deans placed emphasis on speed and acceleration in the loose, which fitted in perfectly with the Scottish gameplan of the mid-1980s to play fast rugby with quick recycling of the ball.

When Deans first came into the Scottish side in the late 1970s, it was a team that was ageing and on the wane. That he survived and flourished through the bad days of Scottish rugby is testament to his talent, and the successes of 1984 and then as captain in 1986 were thoroughly deserved.

Deans stepped down from international duty in 1987, after captaining Scotland in the World Cup of that year. He made 37 Five Nations Championship appearances.

with ease, bagging all 18 of Scotland's points with six penalty goals. France suffered the indignity of outscoring the Scots by two tries to nil but still finishing on the losing side.

Scotland's only reverse of the 1986 championship came at the hands of the Welsh at Cardiff Arms Park, 22-15, but there was real joy as the old enemy England were routed at Murrayfield.

The Hastings brothers were the biggest thorns in the English side. Gavin claimed 21 points to break the record he set earlier in the season against France, and his brother Scott scored the final try in a 33-6 victory. England were totally outplayed, Scotland nullifying the strength of the big English pack by playing fast, mobile rugby which at first stunned the visitors, and then destroyed them.

To finish the season Scotland travelled to Ireland, and although the Irish played with greater passion and skill on the day, the Scots squeezed home by 10-9.

Meanwhile, in Paris, France put England to the sword again and ran out 29-10 winners to ensure that the championship was shared with the Scottish.

The Grandest of Slams

To win only the third Scottish Grand Slam in history would be triumph enough,
but to do it at Murrayfield and deprive England of the glory in the same
match, that surely had to be a dream. Not for David Sole and his heroes...

'Scuse me, mate – Derek White, above, and Finlay Calder, below, usually set up attacking position for Chalmers, far right

It might be easy to forget anything but the deciding game at Murrayfield when you look back on the 1990 Five Nations season, but both the combatants on that day, Scotland and England, had played some fine rugby on the way to setting up such a big showdown.

England had outclassed the Irish (23-0) and destroyed the Welsh (34-6) at Twickenham, and also put the French to the sword on their own Paris turf by 26-7, England's second successive win on French soil. Scotland had warmed up for the 1990 Five Nations season with good wins against Fiji and Romania, and given the fact that Scottish coach Ian McGeechan had led the British Lions to glory the previous summer and had the chance to examine the other Home countries' strengths and weaknesses at close quarters, the Scots felt they had an edge.

In short, Scotland came into the season with some confidence, and a settled squad. Indeed, throughout the four matches Scotland played, they used just 16 players, and then only because Derek White picked up an injury in the final game.

That Scottish confidence took something of a dent in the first match against Ireland. The Irish had taken a beating two weeks previously at Twickenham and had a point to prove, and the Scots did not fire on all cylinders, but they still scraped home 13-10, thanks mainly to a pair of tries from White.

The second game of the series was against the French at Murrayfield, a ground on which France had not won since 1978. Losing Alain Carminati, sent off for stamping on John Jeffrey, with the score at just 3-0 to the Scots, did not help their cause and the home side eventually ran out 21-0 winners. The performance against the Welsh in Cardiff was, like in the

> **"In the changing room afterwards, all the guys were absolutely shattered: sitting around, their heads in their hands, with pain and confusion all over their faces. There was nothing to say."**
>
> ENGLAND CAPTAIN
> WILL CARLING

KEY PLAYER 1990

John Jeffrey

Scotland's most-capped flank forward with 40 appearances in a Scottish jersey between 1984 and 1991, John Jeffrey was a driving force in the Grand Slam of 1990.

Nicknamed the "White Shark" because of the way, with his shock of blond hair, he seemed to cruise up to unsuspecting victims and envelop them in a crunching tackle, Jeffrey was as dangerous in attack as he was in defence. Often a Scottish raid would start with a Jeffrey charge straight up the middle with the ball expertly laid back for recycling to the oncoming support. Invariably one of the fastest forwards on the pitch, Jeffrey scored 11 tries for his country, equalling the record for a Scottish forward.

In defence, particularly against England in 1990, Jeffrey was amazingly adept at spoiling the opposition's ball, time and again managing to frustrate attackers by doing enough in the tackle, ruck or maul to ensure the slowest release.

A rugged farmer, Jeffrey was an inspiration to those around him, and a great loss to Scotland's national team when he hung up his boots in 1991.

Irish game, not a convincing one and Wales, fresh from a mauling against England, ran the Scots close. But it was not close enough and they lost 13-9. The Grand Slam was on.

The deciding match at Murrayfield had everything riding on it: the Calcutta Cup, Triple Crown, championship and Grand Slam. Whoever won would take all the prizes.

England, having played some scintillating rugby thus far in the season, were favourites, but the Scots devised the more effective game plan and it started with skipper David Sole walking his team on to the pitch in a slow, purposeful manner which showed they meant business. Jeffrey and his fellow flanker Finlay Calder set about making themselves as troublesome as possible to disrupt England's normally tight forward play, and slowly but surely the English fell apart.

Craig Chalmers kicked two penalty goals to give Scotland a 6-0 lead before Jerry Guscott scored to pull things back to 6-4. Chalmers stretched the lead again just before half-time with another penalty: 9-4.

The steady kicking of fly half Chalmers was no doubt important for Scotland, but equally so was the fact that England's normally deadly accurate full back Simon Hodgkinson missed several chances and that the visitors spurned some other apparently kickable opportunities to put points on the board, opting instead for positional advantage which was not driven

John Jeffrey, the Scottish White Shark, goes on the prowl – and hunts in a pack with his famous back-row colleagues Finlay Calder and Derek White, opposite

The Cup runneth over

The Calcutta Cup has been fought over by England and Scotland since 1879. The previous year, the Calcutta FC in India had been disbanded because there was no other worthwhile team to play. The club, largely run by British Army officers and civil servants, decided that their funds should be used to provide a trophy for an annual competition between England and Scotland. The trophy, made out of the actual rupees withdrawn from the bank, is a tapered cup, with three snake handles and a silver elephant as the lid piece. The inscription on the Calcutta Cup reads:

THE CALCUTTA CUP
PRESENTED TO THE RUGBY
FOOTBALL UNION
BY THE CALCUTTA
FOOTBALL CLUB AS
AN INTERNATIONAL
CHALLENGE TROPHY
TO BE PLAYED
FOR ANNUALLY BY
ENGLAND AND SCOTLAND
1878

"Saturday March 17, 1990, is one of those dates that's engraved in my mind like it was put there with a hammer and chisel. Grand Slam Saturday. The best day of my rugby life. It was the day of the underdog and it was the day that we beat the odds-on favourites for one of the biggest prizes rugby can offer."

SCOTLAND SCRUM HALF
GARY ARMSTRONG

Gavin Hastings

Gavin Hastings was yet another in the line of superb Scottish full backs, following the talented Andy Irvine and Peter Dods and probably outshining all who went before him.

He burst on to the international scene with a stunning debut in 1986, kicking all of Scotland's points in a thrilling 18-17 victory over the French, a record for a Scottish player. It was a mark which did not last long – just weeks later he amassed 21 points against England, and he ended his first Five Nations season with a tally of 51, another record.

Hastings may not have been the quickest of full backs, but his rock-steady defence and bone-jarring tackles bred confidence in those around him, and his bulldozing attacking sorties usually led to a chance being created somewhere in the Scottish line – witness the chip ahead which led to Tony Stanger's winning try in the 1990 Grand Slam decider.

He was made captain of Scotland in 1993 and went on to lead the British Lions in New Zealand. He retired with 61 caps and 667 points, including 17 tries and 140 penalties.

home. England captain Will Carling and pack leader Brian Moore faced a lengthy media inquisition about their decisions in the aftermath. The crunch came early in the second half when Gavin Hastings chipped deftly into England's 22 and winger Tony Stanger followed up to score with the England defence shot to pieces.

The match finished 13-7 to the home side and the whole of Scotland seemed to erupt when the final whistle blew. It was undoubtedly one of Scotland's finest moments and one of the Five Nations' greatest games.

"No one, apart from the 15 Englishmen on the field, can even begin to imagine the numbing helplessness we felt when the final whistle blew. The Scottish crowd swept past us in their crazed rush to capture a glimpse of their heroes, as the untouchables from England were left to find their way off the field as quickly and as anonymously as they could."

ENGLAND FLY HALF
ROB ANDREW

The Last Champions

Scotland started the final Five Nations with few hopes, and ended watching television, waiting for a Welsh Wembley miracle which duly arrived. Having played thrilling rugby inspired by the record-breaking Gregor Townsend, the Scots were deserving champions

The Scottish triumph of 1999 had many heroes, but John Leslie, right, Scott Murray, scoring far right top, and Alan Tait, far right bottom, were outstanding throughout the tournament

A triple Slam for France, or another Triple Crown for England? The odds were on a French-English carve-up when the 1999, and last, Five Nations kicked into gear. While Scotland's coach Jim Telfer might be running his last championship campaign and Wales had Graham Henry making his debut as a Five Nations coach, all the pre-season focus was on whether France could stampede their way to a third successive Grand Slam or England could halt the Gallic train and claim anything more than wins over their Celtic cousins before Italy arrived to join the party in 2000.

Scotland, of course, had other ideas. They had recruited a pair of New Zealand brothers, the Leslies, to add to an already cosmopolitan team and, in Telfer, had the shrewdest coach in the tournament. The omens were still not propitious, however. Scotland had failed to match England's pre-Christmas victory over the previously all-conquering South African tourists, crumbling 35-10 at Murrayfield, and the wooden spoon was expected to find its way north of the border if the Scots could not overcome newly-revived Wales at home in their first match.

Indeed that Welsh match in Edinburgh did set the scene for the rest of the Scots' campaign, thrillingly and unexpectedly. John Leslie, the resolute centre of the two brothers, ripped possession out of shocked Welsh hands straight from the kick-off and galloped over unopposed to score after 10 seconds, the quickest Five Nations try of all time. You would expect a Kiwi to be quick to make an impact on a rugby field.

The rest of the Scottish scorers in a breathtaking 33-20 victory neatly pointed out the players to watch for the rest of the season – Gregor Townsend, Alan Tait and Scott Murray, an athletic, mobile lock forward plucked from Bedford for his Five Nations debut.

Wales actually fought back well from the surprise of conceding such a rapid try and, with a score from wing Dafydd James and help from Neil Jenkins' reliable boot, they were 13-8 ahead at half-time.

After the break, however, it was time for Townsend, fresh from an outstanding season in French club rugby, to make his mark. First he intercepted Jenkins' pass to race 60 metres for a classic poacher's try. Scott Gibbs hit back to

> **"I would like to thank those people who wrote us off because they were the ones who really spurred us on. We did not even rate a mention and that only made us more determined."**
>
> SCOTT MURRAY
> on Scotland's fighting spirit

put Wales in front once again but then Townsend showed just why he was so valuable to the Lions in 1997 with a mini-break which created the space for substitute Tait to crash through and level at 20-20.

With Kenny Logan on strong form with the boot, Scotland sealed victory when Murray ended a four-phase move by crashing over for a well-deserved try. Roll on England.

Clive Woodward's team sat out the first weekend of the championship but they showed no ill effects at Twickenham. Scotland had not won there since 1983 and when Tim Rodber and Dan Luger both blasted through for tries to put England 14-0 up inside 20 minutes, an end to the

run looked unlikely. However, Murray was giving Martin Johnson unexpected trouble in the lineout and after more Townsend magic, Tait grabbed two tries, one a classic charge through the heart of the English defence, and Scotland had pulled back to only 17-14 down.

Full back Nick Beal benefited from some weak Scottish tackling to go over for England's third try, but still Townsend was not finished and he embarrassed Mike Catt into an error which gifted him another breakaway score – 24-21.

Unfortunately the one area of Scotland's game which was malfunctioning was Logan's kicking and, with Jonny Wilkinson

immaculate with the boot, the visitors could not make the final step.

The Scots had their weekend off for the next round of matches, so they could watch Wales's astonishing 34-33

victory in Paris. It was an omen of things to come in more ways than one, but first, with confidence growing, they had to face Ireland at Murrayfield.

The Irish record of one win over Scotland in 14 games looked painfully apt after the home side completed a four-try 30-13 victory despite going 7-0 down after three minutes. That penalty try was almost the limit of Ireland's attacking effort. Wing Cameron Murray soon shrugged off

Forward march –
Doddie Weir, above,
crashes through the
Welsh defence, followed
by Eric Peters, far right,
while Stuart Grimes, far
right top, hits the heights
against England

> "There's a feeling that we ended up as champions because England lost to Wales, but the real reason is that we played positive rugby and won with some style in Paris."
>
> JIM TELFER
> hits back at Scotland's critics

the threats to his place with the first of two tries and with Townsend, inevitably, scoring as well Scotland led 15-10 at half-time.

Cammie Murray grabbed his second try in the second half and then lock Stuart Grimes showed the benefits of dogged support play when he joyfully finished off an exhilarating length-of-the-field move started by Townsend.

England, however, were also winning, having put paid to rag-tag

France 21-10 the same day and it looked like Scotland would be just gallant bit-players in the fourth English Grand Slam of the decade.

Victory in Paris, of course, would draw them level in the Five Nations table on six points with England – who were playing their final game at Wembley the next day – though their record in France was poor, just one win in 14 games.

Little could have prepared the travelling Scottish fans for the game they were about to see in the Stade de France, certainly one of the most extraordinary in the history of the Five Nations. Eight tries were scored in the first half, six of them in an astonishing

22 minutes, as Scotland cut France to pieces and the capacity crowd began to boo the home team, who had been heroes only a year before with back-to-back Grand Slams.

The French actually started in style, with fly half Thomas Castaignède setting up a rapid try for Emile Ntamack, who had already scored a hat-trick in a losing cause earlier in the season against Wales. Unfortunately Castaignède was injured in the process and barely before he had limped off the pitch for treatment – never to return – Scotland were surging ahead.

Townsend was the orchestrator of Scottish dreams, conducting a virtuoso performance which included a try for himself as he became only the fifth man in the history of the tournament to score in every game of a season, and the first since French centre Philippe Sella in 1986.

Tait also bounded over for two scores, taking his total for the championship to five, and flanker Martin Leslie's brilliant support work brought him another two. The second half was something of an anticlimax after that, with Scotland managing only one penalty to stretch their winning margin to 36-22, but it was still their biggest victory ever over France. So, basking in the glow of that performance,

Scotland sat back to watch Wales play England in the hope that their Celtic brethren would do them an unexpected favour and secure their first win over the English in six games.

England dominated and were in front after only three minutes when winger Luger went over for a try. Debutant wing Steve Hanley also scored and Richard Hill added a third, but all the time Jenkins was keeping his side in touch with penalties and when full back Shane Howarth went over, Wales pulled level at 25-25. Wilkinson slotted two penalties but that merely set up the amazing climax.

Two minutes into injury time Welsh and Scottish fans erupted as one when Scott Gibbs crashed through almost the entire English defence to score near the posts. All Jenkins had to do was kick the conversion. Wales would win 32-31 and the championship would be Scotland's. You can rely on Jenko.

Scott Murray

Bedford's Scott Murray brought a new dimension to lock forward play in his first season in the Five Nations. Comparatively light for a second row at 16st 7lbs, Murray called on the skills he learnt as a Scottish Schools basketball international and proved so effective against his heavyweight and more illustrious opponents that he turned the lineout into one of Scotland's key attacking platforms.

While he was also an excellent scrummager, it was not just in the set piece that the former Edinburgh Accies player excelled. His athletic build allowed him to cover huge ground to win possession for the Scots and support their exciting back play.

Murray had been plucked almost from obscurity for the 1999 championship. He made his Scotland debut in a traumatic 37-18 defeat by Australia in '97 and, while his try in that game promised much, he only won two caps in the next two years. His move south to Bedford was not received well by the selectors, but they made the right choice for the final Five Nations campaign: Murray ended the season as the player of the tournament.

Ireland

Everybody loves the Irish, and not only because of the riotous pleasures of a Five Nations weekend in Dublin. If you can remember you were there, you'll know you saw one heck of a game the like of which will keep the tournament alive, alive'o for many years to come

Conor McGuinness displays the dejection too often seen on Irish faces at the end of a Five Nations campaign

BY
KEITH WOOD

'In one beautiful moment, it encapsulated the famous Irish spirit'

Keith Wood's Five Nations record reads: Played 11, Won 1, Lost 10. Only one glorious triumph for the swashbuckling hooker, and an awful lot of heartbreaking defeats – three of them by just one point. Yet Ireland's modern-day talisman still loves rugby's oldest international tournament. It's been that way ever since he broke his jaw on the rockery...

Rugby has always been a huge part of my life. As a youngster growing up in a small town in County Clare, it shouldn't have been. Killaloe is hurling country. However, ours was a rugby household. My father played 29 times for Ireland and a couple of times for the Lions and both my brothers played senior rugby.

Like every child, we played and loved whatever was on the television at any given time. We played tennis during Wimbledon, soccer during the World Cup, we even jumped fences in our garden during the show-jumping championships. But the be all and end all for us was the Five Nations Championship.

My brother John and I used to kick the crap out of each other on the lawn, much to the distress of my mother, who quite liked the lawn. And that is where my first memory of the Five Nations lies: a spectacular chip over my brother's head followed by an outrageous dive and a cracked jaw in the rockery. But it was worth it 'cos Ireland won.

But the real-life rugby stories are much better. My memories are those of a young man. I never witnessed the exploits of Karl Mullen's great side of the late 1940s or

knew the wizardry of Mike Gibson or of all the heroes in between. The Five Nations sparks for me have been in the 1980s and '90s: Locky's tug-like impression as he steamed to the line with a multitude of English forwards on his back; the unerring boot of Ollie Campbell, breaking the Scottish hearts in '82; Michael Kiernan's drop goal for Triple Crown victory, Nocl Mannion's 50-yard dash against Wales that left a country breathless; Michael Galway's cracking late try against England in '93 which, in one beautiful moment, encapsulated the famous 'Irish spirit'.

The Five Nations competition is an institution in Ireland. It is not just part of the sporting calendar, it is an integral part of Irish life. Dublin comes alive with the sights and sounds of the Scottish ballads, the Welsh choirs, the English chariots and the French panache.

Even in this barren spell of 14 years, demand for tickets is phenomenal. World giants of the southern hemisphere just about fill Lansdowne Road, but a championship match could be sold out twice over. The Five Nations has an intangible quality to draw people from far and wide. For Ireland the '99 championship neither flattered nor deceived

Keith Wood, opposite, often ends up black and blue for Ireland

Follow me, boys – Paddy Johns leads out the Irish against Wales at Wembley. They won there in '99, but sadly Lansdowne Road, opposite, while a favourite haunt of visiting fans, has too infrequently been the scene of Irish triumphs

anyone. A gut-wrenching loss to France foretold of great possibilities. A Triple Crown perhaps? A sparkling 60 minutes of rugby against Wales added credence to that dream. We won, but a 20-minute purple patch by the Welsh showed up some of our frailties. From this promising position it all went horribly wrong. Physically mauled by a superior English pack on the day and comprehensively outfoxed by Gregor Townsend's genius, our dreams were dashed on the rocks. The Scots were crowned deserving champions, the French got an unlikely wooden spoon and the rest of us were left to dwell on an 'almost' season. Our narrow loss against the French didn't seem so heroic now, but our

> "Dublin comes alive with
> the sights and sounds
> of the Scottish ballads,
> the Welsh choirs,
> the English chariots and
> the French panache."
>
> KEITH WOOD
> on the Five Nations circus

victory over the Welsh was outstanding. In total, absolute confusion, the beauty of the Five Nations – any team can beat any other team, and often do.

But now that the line-up has changed, how will the tournament fare? The Five Nations is a marvellous competition as it stands, but it would be presumptuous and arrogant of us to want to keep it that way to the exclusion of rapidly improving European teams.

Italy has deserved inclusion for many years now. Their international team have greatly improved, beating Five Nations sides regularly over the last few years. Their entry adds another little bit of spice to an already intriguing competition. The Five Nations has a very

bittersweet feeling with me. I love it, the intensity, the historic rivalries, the traditions. They are unique, a situation the southern hemisphere teams would die for.

But personally, in terms of success, the tournament has been less than favourable to me. My first win came against Wales at Wembley in '99. I played my first Five Nations match in '95.

Yet after all those years of disappointment, I love it all the more. It must be the masochist in me. Months after breaking my duck, I can still feel the glow of success emanating from that one win. Just one win! God only knows how I would react if we were to win the championship.

KEITH WOOD'S ALL-TIME IRELAND FIVE NATIONS XV

After many hours' soul-searching, Keith Wood wrote: "When asked to form my best ever Irish XV, I really struggled. My tender years leave me quite inadequate for the job, my frames of reference are a bit narrow. So in order to compensate, I had to pick a team from the 1990s that I feel Ireland could be proud of. I have gone for guys I have played with or against. Apologies for some biased selections."

Brendan Mullin, above, and Malcolm O'Kelly, right, won Keith's vote in a difficult choice of players at centre and lock

15 Jim Staples (Full back)
I'll start at the top – the position I know best: full back. Although Ciaran Clarke had some good moments in the green and Conor O'Shea has improved out of sight, I would have to opt for Jim Staples. Plagued by injury, Jim always came back for more and his hitting of the line was second to none.

14 Simon Geoghegan (Right wing)
11 Keith Crossan (Left wing)
On the wings I go for two very different characters. Simon Geoghegan would make it on anyone's side – his frantic running style, shock of blond hair, and appetite for work offered something a little bit special. And Keith Crossan from Instonians would sneak in past some of the younger lads. Even though he was near the end of his career at the start of the 1990s, Keith's scurrying figure always seemed to notch up some tries, and get the crowd going.

12 Philip Danaher (Centre) Captain
13 Brendan Mullin (Centre)
The centres are very difficult, especially with some great performances recently by Kevin Maggs, but I would have to go with my first club captain, Philip Danaher, and Brendan Mullin. Brenny had the silky skills to finish off plays, and is the record Irish try-scorer, while Philip always seemed to take control of proceedings and keep us on track.

10 Eric Elwood (Outside half)
Even though David Humphreys has become a hugely influential figure, I am drawn by the quiet man from the West. Images of Eric being chaired off the pitch at Lansdowne after the historic victory against England in '93 are a testament to the control he often brought to bear on games and the esteem in which he is held.

9 Fergus Aherne (Scrum half)
On sentiment I have to give the No 9 berth to the scrum half who played when I was first involved in '92, Gus Aherne. He just edges out Michael Bradley, one of the few winners of a Triple Crown to play a large part in the '90s.

1 Nick Popplewell (Loosehead prop)
Nick is one of the heroes in Irish rugby folklore. His powerful surges and great tight play must put him down as one of the best Irish looseheads of all time.

2 Stevie Smith (Hooker)

At hooker there are a) a young scamp from Clare, b) a very durable and aggressive Corkman, Terry Kingston, who never got injured and left me with splinters in my arse from the subs' bench, and c) the big quiet man from Ballymena, Stevie Smith.

3 Paul Wallace/Peter Clohessy (Tighthead prop)

I have to sit on the fence for our tightheads. I am incapable of choosing Paul Wallace over Peter Clohessy or vice versa. Wally's scrummaging and lineout work are incredible but so are Claw's. Claw's tackling and workrate are phenomenal but so are Wally's.

4 Jeremy Davidson (Lock)
5 Malcolm O'Kelly (Lock)

We were blessed in the '90s with outstanding second-rowers. Michael Galway, Gabriel Fulcher, Paddy Johns and Neil Francis would make it into nearly any team. Paddy in particular, with more than 50 caps to his name, is a cracking player. However, I think the young guns Jeremy Davidson, superb with the British Lions in South Africa in 1997, and Malcolm O'Kelly are and will continue to be in a different league.

6 Philip Matthews (Blindside flanker)
7 Pat O'Hara (Openside flanker)
8 Eric Miller (No 8)

The back row throws up a load of contenders, such as Gordon Hamilton, Victor Costello, Denis McBride, Brian Robinson. Dion O'Cuinneagain, the new Irish captain, will definitely be in the next decade's list, but I have gone for the following. A man plagued by injury during his career takes his place on the open side, although not a true No 7. Pat O'Hara was an inspiration. His never-say-die attitude and the manner in which he put his body on the line made him perhaps my biggest role model in Irish rugby. The blindside spot can only have one real holder – Phil Matthews. He was a big, mean No 6 who made his presence felt all over the pitch. The final spot goes to the youngest Lion in '97, who showed unseen dynamism in the Irish No 8 position – Eric Miller.

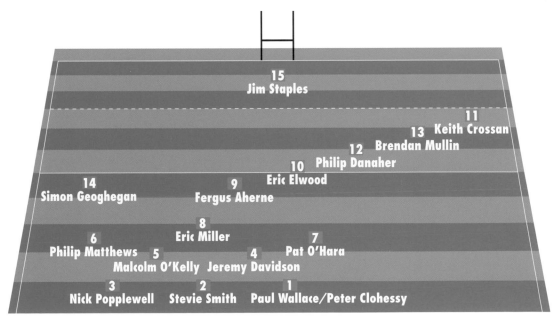

15 Jim Staples

11 Keith Crossan
13 Brendan Mullin
12 Philip Danaher
10 Eric Elwood

14 Simon Geoghegan
9 Fergus Aherne

8 Eric Miller

6 Philip Matthews
7 Pat O'Hara

5 Malcolm O'Kelly
4 Jeremy Davidson

3 Nick Popplewell
2 Stevie Smith
1 Paul Wallace/Peter Clohessy

The One and Only

Out of the post-War years came a side ready to deliver Ireland's golden age in the Five Nations, starting with the country's first and, so far, only Grand Slam season

W E Crawford, above, led the Irish to a share of the Five Nations title in 1926 despite defeat by Wales in Swansea, below

The International Championship, restored to its full complement of five nations with the return of France for the first time since 1931, started again in '46-'47, and the Irish record of two wins and two defeats that season gave little indication of what lay ahead for the men in green.

What was noticeable, however, was the nucleus of a championship-challenging team beginning to take shape around a solid pack and the superb talents of Jack Kyle at fly half. So, though still underdogs, Ireland opened the 1948 Five Nations on New Year's Day in Paris with considerable optimism.

They played to their strengths, and their two flying wingers Barney Mullan and Bertie O'Hanlon, who had made his debut in the 22-0 destruction of England the previous season, were potential match winners. Indeed, Mullan registered one of Ireland's three tries as they ran out 13-6 winners, the country's first victory over France since 1929 and only the second time they had crossed the French try line in Paris on three occasions in a game.

Ireland then went to Twickenham and once again managed to run in three tries. The final scoreline of 11-10 in favour of Ireland belied the fact that the Irish dominated much of the game, thanks largely to aggressive work in the loose by the pack. It marked a third win in a row over England, including two on English soil.

With two home matches in the campaign to come, the Irish started to believe that the Triple Crown and Grand Slam were within reach. The next game was against Scotland at Lansdowne Road, and it proved a comfortable win for the Irish, 6-0. That victory assured Ireland of the championship title, but a win over Wales and the real prizes would be theirs, too. The Ravenhill ground in Belfast was

> "We were well aware of the tension and air of expectation in the crowd and indeed throughout the whole country. I felt we could win and I think that was the general feeling among the players. There was the psychological factor of not having won the Triple Crown for almost half a century and that imposed its additional burden. But to counter that, we felt this was the golden chance and that it must not be missed."
>
> IRISH CAPTAIN KARL MULLEN on the Grand Slam decider with Wales

Ireland – the early years

The slow starters of the Home Unions, Ireland claimed just one outright Five Nations title prior to the Second World War.

Ireland had not posed a powerful force in the days running up to the formation of the Five Nations. Three Triple Crown successes in the 1890s and a share of the title with Wales in 1906 were the highlights of Irish rugby against the other Home nations.

Following the enlargement of the championship to five teams in 1910, Ireland scored an early success with a share of the title with England in 1912, but from then until the end of the Second World War, further triumphs were scarce.

In the 1920s Ireland and Scotland shared the championship in 1926 and then again in 1927, but an outright title still evaded the men in green. France's eviction from the championship

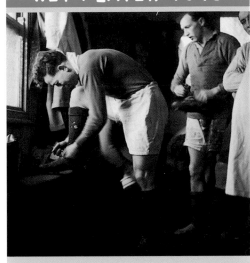

1926: The Irish team at Swansea before the match with Wales

in 1932 until after the war because of player payments, meant Ireland were unable to register a Five Nations triumph until the latter end of the 1940s, but during the pre-War years the Irishmen did manage to share the title in 1932 with England and Wales, and then again in 1939 with the same two countries.

In between, though, came a season to savour, an outright Home nations title in 1935.

Ireland came into that campaign on the back of three defeats in three championship games the previous season. Fielding an inexperienced side for the opening match of 1935 against England – the vast majority of the team had fewer than 10 caps apiece – the Irish probably were not surprised to lose 14-3, but the young side did show promise at Twickenham that would blossom in the ensuing games.

Two weeks later at Lansdowne Road, the youngsters came good by running in four tries in a 12-5 victory against Scotland. This was followed up with a 9-3 win against Wales at the Belfast ground, Ravenhill. It was the first time in 12 matches that the Irish had prevented the Welsh from registering a try.

With reigning champions England, who had drawn with Wales at Twickenham, losing 10-7 to Scotland a week later at Murrayfield, Ireland's win over Wales secured the championship title by a single point.

the venue for the crunch game, and it was packed to bursting with 30,000 eager to see Ireland crowned Grand Slam kings.

It was a close game. Mullan opened the scoring with a try laid on by Kyle, but Bleddyn Williams levelled the scores at 3-3 by half-time. The second half was a tense affair but Ireland gained territorial control and a try by prop forward Chris Daly was the only score of the second 40 minutes, enough to give Ireland their first Triple Crown since 1899 and their first, and still only, Five Nations Grand Slam.

KEY PLAYER 1948

Jack Kyle

In Irish rugby history, the late 1940s are commonly referred to as the "Jackie Kyle era" such was the prodigious fly half's influence between 1947 and 1958 when he accumulated 46 caps.

In his book *Giants of Irish Rugby*, Jack Scally says of Kyle: "He made every rugby pitch he graced a theatre of dreams, dwarfing all who trailed in his wake as he scythed through the defence. In full flight his hand-off gesture was like a royal dismissal to bewildered opponents reduced to look like oxen on an ice rink."

Kyle was just about the complete fly half. His one self-admitted weakness was that he wasn't the greatest tackler. But with the ball in his hands he was untouchable. An attacking runner capable of winding through the tightest defences, Kyle also had superb tactical awareness and could open up a side almost at will with a well-placed kick.

He was the inspiration behind Ireland's championship successes in 1948, 1949 and 1951, and his talents were also recognised by the British Lions, for whom he was capped on six occasions.

A Second Triple

After a disappointing opening to 1949 against
France, the Irish, inspired by Jack Kyle and Jim McCarthy,
rallied to land back-to-back Triple Crowns

KEY PLAYER 1949

Karl Mullen

Karl Mullen remains Ireland's most successful captain, having steered his team to the 1948 Grand Slam, a Triple Crown in 1949 and a championship win in 1951.

He made his Ireland debut in 1947 and went on to play for his country 25 times. He also captained the British Lions in Australia and New Zealand in 1950.

Although a superb hooker and a sound tactician both on and off the pitch, Mullen was best recognised for his man-management skills.

He seemed to have the priceless ability to get the best out of his players, and was the reason behind the fantastic team spirit which carried his side to great things. And yet when he took charge of the Irish team in 1948, he was only 21 years old.

A rare moment of expansive play in an otherwise tight struggle between Ireland and England in 1951

Ireland came into the 1949 campaign still high on their achievements of the previous season, and were justifiably made favourites to dispatch France in the opening match in Dublin. But that is not a mantle worn well by Ireland, and France cantered to victory 16-9, their third successive win on Irish soil.

The men in green raised their game for the next encounter, again at Dublin, against England. The Irish forwards stoked up the passion that had been so powerful in the 1948 Grand Slam and England were swept aside 14-5, the Irish running in two tries.

Back-row forward Jim McCarthy proved the inspiration in the next match, at Murrayfield. Not only was he a superb linkman for fly half Jack Kyle, he was also an aggressive breakaway player capable of penetrating defences. And against Scotland he was at his rampant best, scoring both Ireland's tries as they triumphed 13-3.

Thus a second successive Triple Crown beckoned, with only Wales at Swansea to overcome. Once again, the Irish momentum centred around the partnership of McCarthy and Kyle, and the latter set up the former for the only try of the game with a deft kick to the Welsh line. Full back George Norton converted and the Irish took a half-time lead of 5-0 which they held throughout the second half despite some fiery Welsh attacks.

So the Irish achieved their first back-to-back Triple Crown triumph, a feat they are still waiting to repeat.

Champions Again

The Irish signed off their golden era by taking a third
Five Nations title in four years. With a little more luck, and
better kicking, a second Grand Slam would have been theirs

A single injury probably cost Ireland a second Grand Slam in 1951. They had opened the campaign well enough, beating a resurgent French side by a point, 9-8, at Lansdowne Road. This season was something of a turning point for the French, who matched Ireland in winning three games out of four.

In front of their Dublin crowd again against England, the Irish squeezed out a narrow 3-0 win, thanks to a penalty goal by Des McKibben. It was the first time since 1921 that Ireland had failed to score a try against the English. The third game of the series was against Scotland at Murrayfield and followed much the same pattern as Ireland's previous matches, another narrow win, again by a single

point, 6-5. But this was a more passionate affair as Ireland played much of the match with 14 men after full back George Norton suffered a shoulder injury which not only ruled him out of the final game against Wales, but also ended his rugby career.

And how Ireland missed Norton's kicking talents in the match which could have brought a second Grand Slam in four seasons. Despite several chances, including a conversion attempt after a superb Jack Kyle try, Ireland did not land one kick at goal, and were held, frustratingly, 3-3. It was enough to secure the title by a point, but the Triple Crown and Grand Slam were tantalisingly out of reach. Five Nations success would remain so for the next 23 years.

On the wagon – Irish players prepare for a rail trip

KEY PLAYER 1951
Desmond O'Brien

From his debut in 1948 at No 8 to his year of captaincy in 1952, Desmond O'Brien was a fixture in the Irish side, and a key member of the team through the country's most successful years.

O'Brien made a position for himself as the right-hand man of captain Karl Mullen, serving as a more than useful pack leader and offering effective tactical guidance from the back of the scrum. He was also an attacking force, his tall, gangly frame making him an awkward proposition, and one try in 20 internationals was scant reward for his skilful running.

After his job moved him to Wales in 1950, O'Brien fought his way into the Cardiff first team and sharpened his defensive game which came to the fore in combination with flankers Jim McCarthy and Bill McKay in the championship-winning side of 1951. So miserly was the Irish back row that the team conceded just four tries in the campaign. O'Brien was asked to lead the Irish team in the 1952 season, after which he retired with 20 caps.

Lansdowne Road is packed to see Ireland beat England for the fifth time in six years on their way to the 1951 title

Success at Last

After a barren spell lasting 23 long years, the Irish were
led back to the top of the Five Nations Championship
by their indomitable Lion, Willie John McBride

reland's agony at coming so close to a second Grand Slam in 1951 can only have been exacerbated in the ensuing years as further success eluded the men in green season after season.

After the heights of 1951, Ireland reached great depths, none worse than the possession of the championship wooden spoon for four out of the five seasons from '58 to '62, including in each of the first three seasons of the 1960s.

Highs through the 1950s and 1960s were few and far between, with three wins out of four and defeat only against rampant Wales in the 1969 season the pinnacle of two decades of championship rugby.

So come 1974, with a side now missing truly great players such as Tom Kiernan, and the Irish were not considered as likely challengers for the championship. Even less so when their campaign began inauspiciously against

Tom Kiernan, top
and right, was an Irish
stalwart for 13 years
from 1960 and sadly just
missed out on their '74
triumph under Willie John
McBride, opposite

Mike Gibson

Meticulous, single-minded and an avid disciple of the training field, Mike Gibson had to wait a long time to taste glory in an Irish jersey. He made his debut for Ireland in 1964 and in a 15-year career garnered 69 caps.

Gibson started his rugby life as a fly half, attracting the attention of the Irish selectors while a student at Cambridge University.

In the late 1960s he switched to the centre and proved a major asset to the midfield. His vision, speed of thought and quickness of foot ensured he was an incisive attacker, and his reading of the game meant he had the uncanny knack of turning up in the right place at the right time.

When Gibson retired in 1979, he did so as the most-capped player in the world, and he is still the Irish appearances record holder. But, more than that, he had secured a reputation which places him among the all-time greats.

France. Led by Willie John McBride and featuring a new cap in second-row giant Moss Keane, the Irish lost 9-6 in Paris. But things would only get better.

Wales at Dublin was the second match of Ireland's 1974 campaign and it was a gritty, defensive performance by McBride's pack in tough conditions that kept the Welsh out after half-time and ensured a 9-9 draw. McBride considered his team unfortunate not to win but was optimistic of the two games to come. "We should definitely have beaten Wales and I was confident about our journey to Twickenham," he said later. "I felt we had a great chance of beating England."

And beat England they did, comprehensively. The 26-21 scoreline in favour of the men in green was Ireland's highest ever score against England and the victory should have been even more comfortable but for the unerring kicking of England's Alan Old, who landed five penalties and a conversion to keep England in sight of the Irish to the end.

The architect of Ireland's win was centre Mike Gibson, who scored two of the team's four tries. McBride said of Gibson: "He was at his brilliant best, and that was incomparable at that stage of his career. England just did not have a man of comparable quality behind the scrum that day."

In Ireland's final game of the season, the Scots were narrowly beaten 9-6 at Lansdowne Road, which left an agonising two-week wait for the Irish to see if either Wales or France would overhaul their five-point total.

In the end, neither side managed to secure the win which would have leapfrogged them above Ireland in the table, and the championship returned to Dublin for the first time since 1951.

Campbell's Crown

In 1982, inspired by their prolific fly half, Ireland reversed their dismal performance of the previous season to claim their first Triple Crown for 33 years

The 1982 season was a topsy-turvy affair compared with what had happened just 12 months before. France, the reigning Grand Slam champions, plummeted to a share of the wooden spoon with just one win in four games. It was a crucial victory, though, because it came against the Irish, who went from four defeats in four in 1981 to three wins and a solitary reverse in 1982. It meant the Triple Crown, but not a second Grand Slam.

> **"I felt that the Irish side's record was totally out of proportion to its ability and experience. Wales was a crucial match, not just in terms of the Triple Crown and championship, but for the future."**
>
> IRELAND CAPTAIN
> CIARAN FITZGERALD

Ireland came into the campaign on the back of seven successive defeats, the country's worst sequence of results for 20 years. Ollie Campbell was a controversial selection at fly half having rested all winter and seen his primary challenger for the No 10 shirt, Tony Ward, do all that was asked of him and more in the run-up to the championship.

Led by Ciaran Fitzgerald at hooker, Ireland opened against Wales at Dublin. They started badly, and at one stage trailed 9-4, but Fitzgerald's forwards took control and Campbell started to weave his magic, setting up two tries for Moss Keane and slotting three kicks himself, as Ireland ran out winners 20-12.

The second hurdle for Ireland was at Twickenham against the English, who were still fielding much of the 1980 Grand Slam side. The real battle came up front, and

Captain Ciaran Fitzgerald, above, wing Trevor Ringland, right, and lock Moss Keane were vital to Ireland's run of success in the 1980s

the Irish forwards were at their very best, eclipsing their English counterparts in virtually all departments.

Campbell was again in sparkling form, and the Irish did enough to secure a rare victory at the English HQ by a single point, 16-15.

With two wins in the bag and Scotland at home in the third match, Irish supporters allowed their thoughts to turn to the very real possibility of a Triple Crown.

On a grey day at Lansdowne Road, the Scots fell into the trap of conceding kickable penalties, and Campbell punished them for it. He bagged all the Irish points with six

KEY PLAYER 1982

Ollie Campbell

If one player deserved to be singled out of the Irish team in 1982 it was Ollie Campbell. His individual tally of 21 points against Scotland in a championship total of 46 (equalling his own record of 1980) was the cornerstone of Irish success.

Campbell made his first appearance in an Irish shirt in 1976 against Australia, but it was not until the 1980s that he was assured of his place over another mercurial Irish No 10 talent, Tony Ward.

He played 22 Tests for Ireland and seven for the British Lions and his total of 217 points for his country (including only one try) were testament to the hours he would spend in solitary practice, kicking goal after goal. There was more to the Campbell game than kicking – he was a calm decision-maker at half back, and an instinctive runner who could unleash an aggressive threequarter move at the blink of an eye.

After an illness in 1984 took him out of the reckoning for the Irish side, Campbell retired with his legend intact.

penalties and a drop goal, and although the game was by no means a classic for the spectators, the 21-12 score in favour of Ireland meant their fans could go home happy.

That the fairytale was brought to a disappointing end in Paris, where the French won 22-9, should not take the gloss off a fine season for the Irish, a year in which they went from whipping boys to Triple Crown champions.

"The crowd were magnificent. They kept singing 'Molly Malone' and 'Cockles and Mussels' throughout the second half as if we'd already won. It lifted us enormously. When the referee blew, I felt ecstatic. Life has never been the same since."

OLLIE CAMPBELL
on the joys of securing the Triple Crown

Bouncing Back

Only the Irish could follow a dispiriting Five Nations whitewash
with a glorious Triple Crown triumph and in 1985 Fitzgerald's boys
did just that, finishing with an extraordinary win over England

Michael Kiernan, right, and Brendan Mullin, far right, proved vital points scorers in 1985, but Tony Ward, who played in '84 and '86, could only sit and watch the title win

The Triple Crown of 1982 was followed by further Irish success when three wins and a defeat against Wales the next season ensured a shared championship title with France. Which makes Ireland's plummet to a whitewash in 1984 – a truly miserable year – even more surprising. Given their record for the unpredictable, perhaps it was obvious what would happen to the Irish in 1985 – of course they won the title again, and in style under the guidance of Ciaran Fitzgerald.

This was one of Ireland's best ever seasons. The men in green did not lose a game, and finished the Five Nations as the highest scoring team, with the second best defence in the series.

Against Scotland the Irish rescued a win with a thrilling finale. Scottish full back Peter Dods had kicked his country into a 15-12 lead with just four minutes remaining, but Fitzgerald's troops stormed back from the restart and a superb move in the back line opened up the chance for winger Trevor Ringland to cross the Scottish try line for the second time in the game with just a minute of time to go. Michael Kiernan converted, Ireland won 18-15 and were off and running.

A bad-tempered match in Dublin against France produced a 15-15 draw, courtesy mainly of French disregard

> "The fervent, often frantic business of playing with the heart as well as the head carried Ireland to another defiant triumph in Dublin. Ireland won a heart-stopping match in little short of epic style."
>
> JOHN MASON – DAILY TELEGRAPH on the Irish win over England

What a Silly Tucker

The France v Ireland match programme for 1980 caused much merriment in the Irish dressing room. Back-row forward Colm Tucker found that his surname had been misspelt with an initial 'F'.

Basil Maclear, an English-born army officer capped 11 times by Ireland as a threequarter between 1905 and 1907, always wore white kid gloves when he played.

Thomas Gordon, an Irish international threequarter who won three caps in 1877-78, had only one hand.

Ireland found they were two players short when they arrived in Cardiff for their 1884 international against Wales. Rather than call the game off, they 'borrowed' two Welsh players. So D J Daniel (Llanelli) and F Purdon (Newport) had the unique record of playing for both Wales and Ireland.

Ciaran Fitzgerald

As a hooker Ciaran Fitzgerald was technically sound. In the rucks and mauls he could be a ferocious ball winner. But it was as a captain of his country that Fitzgerald excelled.

In 25 appearances for Ireland he led them on 19 occasions – and with two Triple Crowns and a shared championship to his credit, the success he brought to the Irish people secured him a place in Ireland's rugby folklore.

Fitzgerald's greatest assets as a captain were his refusal to panic in the face of adversity and an ability to keep his players' minds on the job in hand at times when they could have been swept away on the tide of emotion which always surrounds a successful Irish team.

If there is a single blot on the Fitzgerald copybook it is his captaincy of the British Lions, for which he was chosen following the Five Nations in 1983. His team were blown away by the All Blacks and the captain took most of the blame.

That he bounced back in 1985 to lead the Irish to yet more glory speaks volumes for the man.

for the laws of the game. Kiernan kicked five penalties from his seven attempts, while the visitors grabbed a couple of converted tries and a penalty goal. With Wales dispatched 21-9 in Cardiff, a home match with England was left between the Irish and the Triple Crown.

The season had not been a good one for England, with only one win, over Scotland, and a draw against France in the credit column. But against Ireland there followed an epic game decided only in the last minute. England opened the scoring early on through a Rob Andrew penalty, but the young English fly half then squandered his next three attempts at goal and Ireland went ahead through a Brendan Mullin try after the centre charged down an English clearance kick.

A Kiernan penalty gave Ireland a 7-3 half-time lead which was wiped out in the 55th minute by a Rory Underwood try and another Andrew penalty. England led 10-7. It was an advantage they held until seven minutes from time when Kiernan kicked his second penalty, and Irish passions began to soar. With just a minute left Ireland won a lineout deep in enemy territory and Kiernan calmly slotted a drop goal. The game was up for England, and the Triple Crown Ireland's once more.

England

Whether champions or wooden spoonists, the English have always been the team to beat for the other four nations, but that has not stopped them collecting more Grand Slams and Triple Crowns than any of their rivals

"I'm scrubbing up quite nicely, don't you think?" England's 1922 team take a half-time grooming break at Cardiff

BY
BILL BEAUMONT

'The Five Nations is the fabric of our life'

Bill Beaumont restored England's credibility when he led them to their first Grand Slam for 23 years in 1980. Capped 34 times and captain for 21 matches, the lock forward also led the British Lions in South Africa. He may have lost on his Five Nations debut, but from the moment he saw his first game as an 11-year-old, the tournament has had a special place in his heart...

The first Five Nations match I ever saw was in 1964. My school rugby team played a match in Edinburgh on the Friday afternoon, and we stayed over to see the Calcutta Cup match. We arrived at Murrayfield at midday on the Saturday and plonked ourselves down on our seats in the enclosure, soaking up the atmosphere for three hours until the kick-off. It made a deep impression on me, although never for a second did I dream that one day I would play on that pitch. The only black spot on a wonderful day was the result: Scotland won 15-6.

My first Five Nations match – and, indeed, my first full England cap – was against Ireland in 1975, and I remember the thrill of being selected as if it were yesterday. On the Monday before the match I bought an *Evening Standard* outside Olympia tube station to find out the England line-up. I knew there was no possibility of my being in the team because Roger Uttley was certain to be the front lineout jumper. There on the back page of the *Standard* I saw the England team in big bold type and in smaller print underneath the names of the six substitutes. My name was the last of the six in the list and I stood there

> **"The tournament is unique, with years of tradition. It is the friendships you make and the banter between the supporters in the pubs around the cities. Quite simply, I love the Five Nations."**
>
> BILL BEAUMONT
> shows forwards are emotional, too

shaking with excitement, reading it over and over again to make sure it was not a mistake.

When I turned up for training with the England squad, I was greeted by an incredible piece of news. The great Uttley had knackered his back on the train down to London while bending over to pick up a piece of apple pie. It may sound far-fetched but it was true. At seven o'clock on the Friday morning, Alec Lewis the chairman of selectors, came to my bedroom, woke me up, shook me warmly by the hand and said: "Congratulations, you are in the team tomorrow to play Ireland. Good luck." I was in!

We arrived at Lansdowne Road an hour before the kick-off and after I had changed into my kit I spent about half an hour in the loo. I was incredibly nervous and excited, my mind trying to cope with the gamut of emotions. My mind was also trying to prepare for the forthcoming confrontation of the first lineout with Ireland's front jumper. He was a man called Willie John McBride, whose fearsome reputation stretched to every corner of the world. He had just returned from captaining the unbeaten Lions in South Africa and it struck me that

White knight – as an inspiring captain and a barnstorming lock, Beaumont helped England shrug off the dark days of the 1970s

he might not be completely overawed at the prospect of the imminent conflict with W B Beaumont of Fylde – potential one-cap wonder.

I could hardly believe the roar that greeted us as we ran on, but it was nothing compared to the tremendous crescendo of noise that heralded the appearance of the Irish side led by McBride. Eventually the game kicked off and soon we had the first lineout. For the previous five years Willie John had been my idol. At the first lineout I turned to look at him and I remember the disdain and almost contempt with which he glared at me. Before the match Fran Cotton had assured me he was an old man, well past his peak, and he couldn't jump at the best of times, but I soon realised that the king had no intention of being dethroned by me that afternoon. He leaned all over me to win that first lineout and Fran immediately shouted at me to get stuck in or I would be quickly overwhelmed. Shortly afterwards Ireland were on the attack and they threw it to Willie John at the front. I thundered forward and with one hand tapped it down to Jan Webster, who cleared it to touch. The psychological barrier was broken and my particular battle with Willie John ended fairly even.

The speed of the game took me by surprise. The match flashed past in a blur and we lost 12-9 after being 9-6 ahead

with only 10 minutes to go. At the final whistle I was heart-broken, and tears were shed.

At the end of 1977 I was chosen to lead England against the American Eagles at Twickenham, a game we won 37-11. I had never had any ambition to captain England, so I was thrilled when it was announced that I would lead the side in Paris in the first game of the 1978 Five Nations. France were the reigning Grand Slam champions, and our mission would be partly successful if we managed to give them a run for their money. Despite three severe injuries just before half-time, we did well to restrict the defeat to 15-6.

One reason for England's lack of success in the 1970s was the consistently bad selection. But the selectors did eventually strike gold in 1980. Phil Blakeway had only recently returned to rugby after breaking his neck two years before, but his performance at tighthead prop was critical to our Grand Slam. The opening game was at Twickenham against Ireland, the favourites for the championship. Their new fly half Ollie Campbell had emerged as a deadly accurate goal kicker. It was essential for us to destroy the Irish pack or we would be in big trouble. For once, the best-laid plans of mice and men actually came off. With Dusty Hare on fine kicking form, we beat them 24-9.

Two weeks later in Paris, France started with a bang when Jean-Pierre Rives scored a try in the second minute. But our pack reproduced the same driving play that had ripped the heart out of the Irish, we dominated for 70 minutes and then managed to hold on for a 17-13 win. That evening we went with the French players to the Moulin Rouge, where we lapped up the extravagant floor show, and

then went on to one or two nightclubs where some serious gargling was done. The build-up to the England-Wales match was distasteful, sparked off by some irresponsible comments in the newspapers and a supposed war of words between Fran Cotton and Graham Price.

Despite the animosity in the press, I still had little idea of what was going to happen when the match actually started. The opening exchanges were conducted in an unreal atmosphere and the crowd were baying as if they were at a bullfight. At the first lineout there was a bit of a scuffle with elbows going in every direction. The scrums were going down with a frightening ferocity as the front rows charged at each other. After 10 minutes the referee, David Burnett, took Geoff Squire and myself on one side

Paul Ackford, right, was one of Beaumont's successors in the second row who helped restore pride in English rugby

and told us to tell our teams that the next person to commit an act of foul play would be sent off. I gathered everyone together and repeated what I had said in the changing room – that we would win if we concentrated on playing rugby. I warned that the next person to indulge in any rough play would have to be a lunatic. A few minutes later Paul Ringer openly committed a late and dangerous tackle on fly half John Horton and was quite rightly sent off.

With 65 minutes left, I told our team that we could never hold our heads high again if we lost to 14 men. Had Ringer not been sent off, Wales would probably have won. What's more, Dusty Hare kicked the penalty which we were awarded for the Ringer incident and in the end those points made the difference between the two teams. Wales played remarkably well with 14 men and looked to have won the game with a try three minutes from the end which put them 8-6 ahead, but then Dusty converted another penalty with almost the last kick of the match. There were fantastic scenes in the dressing room, even though it resembled a busy casualty department on a Saturday night.

A month later, droves of English fans swept up and down Princes Sreet, Edinburgh, in the most emotional prelude to a game I can recall. Midway through the second half of the match we were leading 23-6, but then the Scots delighted the crowd of 75,000 with some breathtaking running and tries by Alan Tomes and John Rutherford. We clung to our 30-18 lead during a thrilling last ten minutes in which I was aching to hear the final whistle. Suddenly, it went and, lo and behold, we were champions. We had done the lot. We had scored our highest total against Scotland, retained the Calcutta Cup, won the championship, collected our first Triple Crown for 20 years and completed the Grand Slam for the first time since 1957.

It was odd that when the final whistle blew I found myself at that precise moment surrounded by the three guys who had been through all the bad times with me and who would particularly cherish the memories of that unforgettable season: Peter Wheeler, Fran Cotton and Tony Neary. In a spontaneous gesture, Fran and Peter lifted me on to their shoulders and chaired me off the pitch.

Back at the hotel, the team were mobbed all night by ecstatic supporters and the champagne flowed freely. At one stage, though, Fran, Nearo and I slipped away for a quiet drink. We recalled the black days of 1976 when we lost every game and no one wanted to know us. We all savoured that day because we knew it was a once-in-a-lifetime experience.

England winning a Grand Slam in the 1970s or '80s was about as rare as snow in July. It was only when Geoff Cooke and Will Carling took over that England were better organised than most of the other sides. The highlight for me of the early 1990s was the wins they had in Paris – there were some superbly disciplined performances there by England – while winning in Cardiff in 1991 for the first time since 1963 took a huge millstone off English rugby. Dean Richards, Wade Dooley and Paul Ackford were immense during that era, and Rob Andrew always played the right tactic to suit England on the day.

Naturally I was terribly disappointed England lost at Wembley in the 1999 Grand Slam decider, but that is what Five Nations rugby is all about. There was not a lot to choose between the sides, and it was a tremendous tournament.

In the Five Nations, every game is tough. To go to Murrayfield, to go to Cardiff, to go to Paris, to go to Lansdowne Road – regardless of what sort of side you've got, they are hard games. You can't believe how quickly a match goes. Italy coming in gives it another slant and I'm all for that. I think it will be very hard for them to handle a tough game every fortnight. Their resources will be stretched to the limit, but in time they will overcome it.

The Five Nations is the fabric of our life. It's a unique tournament with more than 100 years of tradition. It's the friendships you make and the banter between fans in the pubs around the cities. Quite simply, I love the Five Nations.

Thanks, mate – Roger Uttley's back injury, sustained when he bent over on a train to pick up a piece of apple pie, ensured Bill Beaumont won his first England cap in 1975

BILL BEAUMONT'S ALL-TIME ENGLAND FIVE NATIONS XV

After his personal experience of the Grand Slam triumph in 1980, it is no surprise that Bill Beaumont has plumped for six of the battle-hardened players who saw England back to the good times. He has modestly omitted a certain Fylde lock forward who would make most fans' shortlist for a second row slot, but elsewhere he casts a wide net across the generations to find a fine team blending attacking inspiration with uncompromising competitiveness

15 Bob Hiller (Full back)
He went on two Lions tours and was the leading scorer on both. An outstanding player but would have been better in a stronger England team.

Peter Wheeler, below, Jerry Guscott and Rory Underwood, far right – outstanding players in any era

14 Rory Underwood (Right wing)
You don't get that many caps (85) and score that many tries (49) without being a top operator. He'd have to switch from the left to fit in Mike Slemen.

13 Jerry Guscott (Centre)
I've gone for two attack-minded centres because that's what people want to see. Guscott's defence is all right but I don't think Duckham would put it as top of his priorities – but then I would rather see him scoring tries than making tackles.

12 David Duckham (Centre)
The outstanding England player of the 1970s. When you saw him playing

for the Lions and the Barbarians, that's when you saw the true potential of this man. One of the glamour boys of English rugby but again he didn't play in the best English team.

11 Mike Slemen (Left wing)
A great all-round footballer.

10 Richard Sharp (Fly half)
I can remember him scoring some fantastic tries for England – one

against Scotland in particular in about 1965 where he kept selling dummy after dummy after dummy.

9 Dickie Jeeps (Scrum half)

When you read the books, everybody tells you what an outstanding player this man was, and England haven't been blessed with world-class No 9s.

1 Fran Cotton (Loosehead prop) Captain

Without a doubt the best that I've played with.

2 Peter Wheeler (Hooker)

An outstanding footballer in the modern game. He could throw the ball in and put it on a sixpence. A very competitive player.

3 Phil Blakeway (Tighthead prop)

A great tighthead, he just didn't move – and that's what you want.

4 Maurice Colclough (Lock)

A great scrummaging second-rower.

5 Martin Johnson (Lock)

He would be the No 2 jumper. An outstanding front-of-the-lineout jumper who has really developed his game and is increasingly involved in the loose. A very tough, uncompromising competitor.

6 Peter Dixon (Blindside flanker)

He went on the 1971 Lions tour to New Zealand as an uncapped player and played in three Tests, yet he didn't play for England as often as he should have done. He was an all-round thinker on the game and an outstanding rugby player.

7 Peter Winterbottom (Openside flanker)

In the 1983 Lions he almost played the All Blacks on his own. I think it took him 12 months to recover.

8 Roger Uttley (No 8)

A close choice between him and Dean Richards, but I would go for Uttley as a converted lock who had good hands and was good defensively. Like Dixon, an outstanding reader of the game.

Bob Hiller will be taking my kicks and my captain would be Fran Cotton. If you look at that team, Wheeler could captain the side, Uttley was a successful captain, Hiller captained England, so did Jeeps and Sharp and now Martin Johnson. So there's plenty of captaincy material. But Cotton would probably toss up better than the others!

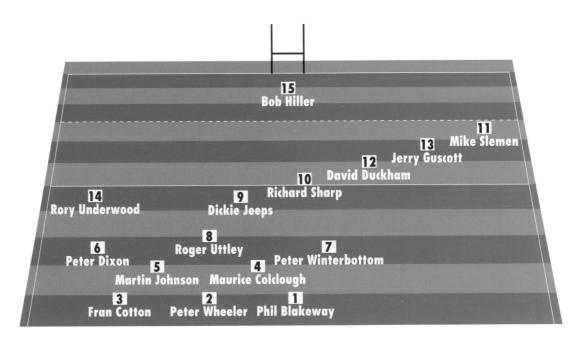

First Blood

A new tournament, the Five Nations, was born in 1910 with the
introduction of France into the annual International Championship of the
Home Unions, and undefeated England were the first to toast the title

Fixtures between all four Home countries began in 1883, marking the start of the International Championship, as it was later to be called. England, whose Rugby Football Union were the controlling influence in the administration of the game, also proved dominant on the field, winning the first two titles.

1910 – Five Nations champions

By the time France joined the tournament in 1910, England had not actually finished top of the pile for 12 years, but they took the honours in the first Five Nations, just as they had in 1883, with three wins and a draw in four matches.

The season was special for England for another reason as it was the first time an international match was held at Twickenham, when they entertained Wales in their opening game of the championship. England won 11-6, and it proved a remarkable debut for winger F E Chapman, who scored a sensational try in the first minute, and also claimed a conversion and a penalty goal.

England then played out a scoreless draw against Ireland at Twickenham before travelling to the Parc des Princes for the first time in a championship match and returning 11-3 victors. Finally, Scotland were beaten 14-5 in Edinburgh.

France's first ever championship season was very much a learning experience. Their defence was fragile, and they conceded 10 tries in their opening match against Wales alone and 22 in total through the championship. In fact, Wales scored a total of 21 tries in the whole series, a record haul.

1912 – Joint champions

England trounced Ireland 15-0 at Twickenham in the 1912 campaign, but they ended up sharing the championship with the Irish after both secured three wins and one defeat apiece.

The English were denied the Grand Slam, Triple Crown and Calcutta Cup by a resilient Scottish side in Edinburgh, going down 8-3.

Wales, the previous year's Grand Slam winners were beaten at Twickenham 8-0, Harlequin centre JGG Birkett scoring on his 21st and final appearance, and France were again dispatched in Paris, this time 18-8.

1913 – England's first Grand Slam

A controversial year for the French at least, crowd trouble at Parc des Princes in the opening match against Scotland earning them a reprimand from the International Board, but for England it was a glorious one, as they improved on their second championship by securing their first ever Five Nations Grand Slam.

Their season started with a first victory in 18 years in Wales, this time in Cardiff, and not only that, but the Welsh were shut out, too, losing 12-0. A second clean sheet of the campaign was then recorded at Twickenham against the French, who were beaten emphatically, 20-0, in a six-try bonanza which included a hat-trick for winger Vince Coates in only his second international.

Ireland were then overcome 15-4 at Lansdowne Road, with two more tries for the prolific Coates, bring to six the number he had scored in his first three internationals.

England clinched the Grand Slam by narrowly beating the Scots at Twickenham, 3-0. A third clean sheet in a remarkable series of matches for the English defence.

1914 – Grand Slam again

If the key to England's success in the 1913 campaign had been the team's stout defence, then the following season was a celebration of try scoring. England ran in 20 tries, only one behind Wales's record haul of 1910, and in all netted 82 points.

The 1914 championship was in fact a tale of two teams. The Welsh pushed England close for the title, scoring 14 tries themselves in their four matches, but Wales's sole defeat of the season came in their opening encounter,

against England at Twickenham where the margin was a mere point, 10-9 to the English.

England scored five tries against Ireland at Twickenham in their second game, winning 17-12. Four more came in Edinburgh against Scotland, including a hat-trick for winger Cyril Lowe, but again the margin of victory could not have been narrower as they won 16-15.

The Grand Slam, though, was wrapped up in style in Paris in the last international match before the outbreak of the First World War. Nine tries, and six conversions by John Greenwood, gave England a 39-13 victory. Lowe scored his second successive hat-trick of tries, but was outshone by his England skipper, Ronnie Poulton Palmer, who crossed the line four times.

Internationals were attracting huge crowds early in the century and here the throng wait expectantly to see Wales play England at Cardiff

Grand Slams Galore

England's team emerged from the War years to collect four
Grand Slams in eight seasons, including back-to-back triumphs
to match their heroes from the previous decade

England had been the team to beat before war broke out in 1914, and although the side of the early 1920s was a new one, it was still the toughest in the championship.

1921 – Grand Slam

The success started in the RFU's golden jubilee year of 1921, with England impressive throughout en route to a third Grand Slam season.

So strong was the England side that it conceded a mere nine points in the four matches, and only one try. This while racking up 61 points, including 13 tries. First Wales (18-3) and then Ireland (15-0) were swept aside at Twickenham, then Scotland had to suffer the indignity of a shut-out on its home turf, going down 18-0.

In Paris France briefly threatened England's Grand Slam chances, narrowly losing 10-6 with Rene Crabos's two penalties the most points England conceded in a single match that campaign. The '21 season was France's best Five Nations performance so far – second in the table with two wins and for the first time managing to score more points than they conceded (33/32).

1923 – Grand Slam

England and Scotland now started a struggle for dominance which would last the rest of the decade. Although England for the fourth time finished the season as Grand Slam

champions, there was, in truth, little to choose between the English and Scottish sides that year. This was certainly no repeat of the all-powerful England performance of two years earlier.

The crunch came at Inverleith in Edinburgh, with Scotland's final game of the championship against England, who still had to play France. A win for Scotland would have meant four wins out of four in the season, while victory for England would set up another Grand Slam chance in Paris.

England achieved their third successive victory on Scottish soil with an 8-6 win, watched by a crowd of some 30,000. Victory in Paris in the final game against France was a formality – the English forwards controlling the game from the outset and providing the platform for a 12-3 win and another Grand Slam triumph.

Wavell Wakefield, top,
England's captain and
key forward during the
success of the 1920s

Brut force and a whiff of victory

Colin 'The Brut' Smart will always be remembered by his England team-mates as the prop forward who brought the sweet smell of success to the Five Nations Championship. During a wild party in Paris to celebrate an England victory over France, Smart was conned into sinking a glassful of aftershave in the belief that it was vintage wine. Bill Beaumont, the England skipper, said: "It caused quite a stink."

Bill Beaumont was England captain the day that Erika Roe made her headline-hitting streak at Twickenham in 1982. "Hey, Bill," scrum half Steve Smith said as Erika bounced bountifully across the pitch, "there's a bird just run on with your bum on her chest."

1924 – Grand Slam

The 1924 season was a high scoring affair in the championship. England, successfully defending a Grand Slam title for the second time, scored 17 tries in their four matches, and in the tournament as a whole, 53 tries were touched down.

Scotland, again, were the main obstacle in England's path and they were also in free-scoring form, recording 12 tries in the season, though they conceded 11.

The Grand Slam-deciding game between England and Scotland at Twickenham was winner-takes-all – it was the last game of the series with both sides sitting on a season's record of played three, won three.

But the game was not the close affair of the previous season. England outplayed the Scots in every department to romp home 19-0. England winger Carlton Catcheside, who had made his debut against Wales in the opening fixture of the campaign, rounded off a remarkable series by running in his sixth try of the tournament, which also meant he had scored in each of his first four international appearances.

1928 – Grand Slam

The mid-to-late 1920s really belonged to Scotland, but the English still managed to increase their Grand Slam tally to six in 1928, although with hardly the ease of some of their previous triumphant campaigns.

Both England's away games in the championship proved close-fought affairs – the Welsh were overcome 10-8 in Swansea, and the Irish narrowly squeezed out in Dublin, 7-6. Wales, in fact, completely outplayed England and should have tasted victory but for one defensive error which let in England winger W J Taylor to score on his debut.

And the Irish actually outscored England by two tries to one at Landsdowne Road, but ultimately fell to their tenth defeat in their last 12 games against the English.

At home England were a stronger proposition, and a leaky French defence was breached four times en route to an 18-8 victory. The Scots, defending their championship title but destined to win only a share of the wooden spoon, were beaten 6-0 to give England their fourth Grand Slam of the decade.

"I say, lads, we really must do something about these shorts." England's Grand Slam team of 1923 can't wait for that Nike clothing contract

Tales of the Unexpected

After only fitful success for 30 years, England suddenly became
unbeatable in the 1957 Five Nations, collecting four wins out of four
in a clean sweep which helped coin the term "Grand Slam"

When England entered the 1957 Five Nations it was on the back of a dismal record since the heady days of the 1920s. In the years after the 1928 Grand Slam, the England roll of honour was bolstered only by three more Triple Crown triumphs –

in 1934, 1937 and 1954 – plus three more championship titles in 1930, 1947 and 1953.

In the 1950s the English had not done much to suggest that they would emerge dominant over the rest of the Five Nations to the extent that they did in 1957. After

England, right, run out for a practice session at the Trinity College ground in Dublin in front of a healthy crowd. The Irish proved a tough obstacle in 1957 for England, top and far right, eventually succumbing 6-0 at Lansdowne Road

KEY PLAYER 1957

Peter Jackson

Coventry and England winger Peter Jackson had an outstanding season for his country in the 1957 Five Nations, scoring three of England's six tries in the series, including a brace against France. By the end of the campaign, he had taken his record to four tries in just seven appearances.

Jackson relied on his outstanding running skills. He was quick and agile, and was known as "The Invisible Man" or "Houdini", such was his ability to slip past defenders in the tightest situations. Another weapon in his armoury was his sheer unpredictability, his changes of direction often bamboozling not only opponents but also his own team-mates.

He made his England debut in 1956, six years after he first appeared in a national trial. An automatic choice throughout 1957, Jackson also helped England to another championship the following season and then toured with the British Lions in 1959 before inexplicably falling out of favour with the England selectors. He played only one more international before earning a Five Nations recall at 32 in 1963.

all, they started the decade by finishing bottom of the table in two successive seasons, 1950 and 1951, managing only one championship win in each campaign.

While 1953 brought the championship and 1954 a Triple Crown, the following season had once again seen the team slump, this time to fourth in the table with only a win and a draw from their four matches.

Come 1957, though, and England were unstoppable. Throughout the series of matches, they made only two changes to their team, a measure of the consistency which was to bring rich dividends. Things started slowly, a 3-0 win at Cardiff Arms Park courtesy of a penalty given away by debutant Welsh winger Keith Maddocks, who crept into an offside position at a lineout and was never again picked by his country.

But from there the England bandwagon slowly gathered pace. A second successive away match saw them travel to Lansdowne Road to meet Ireland, whom England had not beaten on Irish soil for 19 years.

A try by Coventry winger Peter Jackson helped England on their way to a 6-0 win, but

victory was rightly ascribed to an overwhelming performance by the pack, even though they were reduced to seven men after only 20 minutes because of injury.

A 9-5 victory over France at Twickenham meant England secured the championship with still a game remaining, and it also consigned France to the wooden spoon for the first time since 1929, when, like in 1957, they lost all four games in the tournament.

The opponents left that season were Scotland, the old enemy, who came to Twickenham with England hoping to seal a momentous year. The home side continued with their successful strategy of getting the ball out to the backs quickly, and once again it paid off.

Scotland were overrun 16-3, England going over for three more tries to bring their season's tally to six, four of them scored by wingers. The win against Scotland was England's seventh Calcutta Cup triumph in succession, but more importantly it was the country's seventh "Grand Slam" – a term derived from the game of bridge and used by *The Times* for the first time in rugby reporting when it heralded England's 1957 success.

Beaumont's Triumph

After 17 years without an outright championship title and more than 20 without the hint of a Grand Slam, in 1980 Bill Beaumont's vastly experienced side built on the foundations of awesome forward power to fashion a triumphant march through the Five Nations

no championship glory for 17 years and no Grand Slam since 1957 – the England Grand Slam of 1980 marked the end of a long drought in the history of English success in the Five Nations.

The England team was captained by Bill Beaumont, and contained a number of seasoned players hungry for success before their careers came to a close, old warhorses in the pack like Fran Cotton, Roger Uttley, Beaumont himself and Tony Neary, along with some exciting talent in the backs, such as Dusty Hare at full back, John Carleton and Mike Slemen on the wings, and Steve Smith and John Horton paired at half back.

England opened the campaign at Twickenham against Ireland, a team fielding for the first time in the Five Nations a young fly half called Ollie Campbell, who would set an Irish points scoring record with 46 in this campaign. The English game plan was to dominate up front and get among the Irish, using the same principles that had seen the North Division defeat the touring All Blacks earlier in the season. Although England did indeed dominate in the forwards, with Phil Blakeway

"Look, lads, it's like this...we hit 'em hard and we hit 'em early," explains Fran Cotton, top. "Though not with your head, Roger." Uttley, right, was forced off against Wales with this injury after a boot to the head

proving a rock at prop on his debut, after 20 minutes Ireland led 9-3 thanks to three penalties from Campbell.

Forward pressure finally brought its reward, though, and scrum half Smith had the simplest of tasks to touch down for a try, duly converted by Hare, to level the scores. England did not look back from there, and further converted tries from Slemen and No 8 John Scott, plus two penalties from Hare, ensured a 24-9 victory, the most points the English had scored against Ireland for 52 years and equal to the team's tally in the whole of the previous season.

Two weeks later England travelled to the Parc des Princes knowing they had not won on French soil since 1964, but the plan to dominate up front was again a success, although things looked grim when the French captain Jean-Pierre Rives rounded off a typically thrilling move to score in the first minute.

The English forwards soon cranked into gear and their team benefited, with tries for John Carleton and Nick Preston, their first in England shirts, plus two drop goals from Horton moving the visitors into a 17-7 lead. A French attacking storm in the final few minutes was weathered with only a converted try conceded, and another win was tucked away, 17-13.

The clash against the Welsh at Twickenham pitched together the only two

---

"We won so much good ball and kept such a tight control that we destroyed an Ireland side which had been highly rated. When you consider that they were to thrash the Welsh 21-7 at the end of the season, it made a nonsense of their display against us. They were better than that, but they were not allowed to be. That's how we played it that season – with control, not allowing the opposition to play the rugby they wanted."

ROGER UTTLEY
on England's performance against Ireland

KEY PLAYER 1980

Tony Neary

Tony Neary, the wing forward who played his club rugby for Broughton Park and county rugby for Lancashire, was in outstanding form during the 1980 Five Nations campaign.

He made his debut for England in 1971 and in all earned 43 caps for his country. Even given the formidable talent England has produced in the back row since Neary's era, he would still claim a place in most critics' all-time England XV, such was his contribution to the cause.

Neary's greatest asset was his ability to turn defence into attack, tackling oncoming players, ripping the ball clear and driving forward to gain ground. The scourge of opposition fly halves, Neary was also England's most capped international until Rory Underwood surpassed him in 1991.

Bill Beaumont was an inspirational captain for England through the early 1980s and also led the Lions in South Africa

Hooker Peter Wheeler, right, was indomitable in tight and loose for England during their 1980 triumph, while full back Dusty Hare, far right, always ensured opposition mistakes were punished by three points

---

"Bill Beaumont was carried shoulder high from the field and Tony Neary led the champagne celebrations. It was an incredibly emotional affair, especially because so many of the side had known times when a Grand Slam and a Triple Crown had seemed a million miles away."

PROP PHIL BLAKEWAY
after victory over Scotland

---

unbeaten sides in the championship. It was the crunch game, and turned into a torrid match.

Wales, the reigning champions and 27-3 winners over England the season before, outscored the English by two tries to nil and outplayed them too, but three penalty goals from the boot of Dusty Hare ensured a narrow 9-8 victory.

The Welsh lost wing forward Paul Ringer after 15 minutes, sent off for a late and dangerous tackle on Horton, while England flanker Uttley had to withdraw from the game just before half-time with a nasty bleeding head injury caused by Geoff Wheel's boot, and the game degenerated into indisciplined pandemonium.

Battered and bloodied, England had at least emerged victorious and had a month to prepare for the Grand Slam encounter against the Scots at Murrayfield. The power of England's pack proved decisive once again and effectively the Grand Slam was clinched in the first half hour.

Two tries for the dashing Carleton, one created by the elusive running of centre Clive Woodward and the other by the strength of the English scrum, plus a try for Slemen, opened up a 16-0 lead after 30 minutes.

Carleton went on to complete a hat-trick, the first by an English player for 56 years, and, while the Scots fought back bravely after the interval, England ran out 30-18 winners to clinch the Grand Slam and Beaumont was carried shoulder high from the pitch by his delighted team-mates.

Phil Blakeway

The England pack of 1980, so crucial to the Grand Slam triumph, was not short on international experience – Tony Neary won his 40th cap in the opener against Ireland, Roger Uttley his 20th, it was the 21st for Peter Wheeler, the 23rd for Bill Beaumont and the 27th for Fran Cotton.

But Phil Blakeway, the Gloucester prop, was the exception. Ireland was his first cap, but throughout the tournament, Blakeway never looked out of his depth, rather he was the linchpin of the solid performance of the England forwards.

Blakeway's scrummaging at tighthead provided the pivot off which the back row of Uttley, Neary and John Scott could operate so effectively. In particular, in the French game, Blakeway left the opposition scrum in tatters.

What was even more remarkable about Blakeway's Grand Slam campaign was the fact that he sustained a broken rib against France but stayed on the field and also played against Wales just two weeks later. A serious neck injury forced Blakeway into retirement in 1985 – he had already recovered from a broken neck in 1977 – and he finished his playing days with 19 England caps.

Perfectly Packed

The bitter disappointment of Murrayfield 1990 turned to unbridled delight a year later as England, with their forwards once again leading the way, swept to a Grand Slam

ill Carling's England of 1991 emerged with a fierce determination to succeed, a determination undoubtedly forged by their mind-numbing Grand Slam failure of the year before and which translated into a plan of dominating the opposition in set plays, grinding them down and then only occasionally, when the moment was right, spreading the ball to the three quarters.

The campaign began with England having to lay to rest their Cardiff hoodoo, which had seen Wales unbeaten on

After Simon Hodgkinson, top, had kicked his way to a record 60 points and Mike Teague, right, and his fellow forwards delivered possession on a plate, Rory Underwood, far right, and England were able to celebrate a Grand Slam

home soil since 1963. In truth, the Welsh were barely in the game as England dominated both territory and possession.

The winning score of 25-6 included a world-record haul of seven penalties for full back Simon Hodgkinson and a try from flanker Mike Teague, peeling off a scrum near the Welsh goalline.

And so to Scotland, the victors in the clash of the titans 12 months previously at Murrayfield which had seen the Grand Slam go north of the border. This time, at Twickenham, steely England played the percentages and picked the safer options. Fly half Rob Andrew ensured the Scots were kept on the back foot with some deft kicking from hand, and once again Hodgkinson proved his worth as a goalkicker, firing over six from seven to garner 17 of England's 21 points. Nigel Heslop scored the one try of the game as the Scots were beaten 21-12.

Carling's men then travelled to Dublin and secured the Triple Crown by beating the Irish 16-7, their fifth win in a row over the men in green. It was England's toughest match of the campaign and victory only became apparent after a moment of brilliance from

"The whistle and it was all over. What scenes. The relief, the fatigue, the numbness, the pain, the confusion, the crowd, all around, and such joy, such sweet joy."
FLY HALF ROB ANDREW
on the emotions of a Grand Slam triumph

KEY PLAYER 1991

Dean Richards

How England missed their first-choice No 8 in the 1990 season as Dean Richards spent the entire campaign sidelined with injury. The Leicester forward, who made his England debut in 1986, was also injured coming into the 1991 Five Nations. His absence would have been telling.

Richards is a one-off in the history of world-class No 8s. He despised training, preferring to play as much as possible to retain match fitness, and looked downright ungainly as he lolloped across the pitch, socks inevitably around his ankles.

But image is not everything and Richards was a colossus for England. His streetwise common sense and tactical appreciation for the game ensured he always appeared exactly where he was needed, and he possessed a fine pair of hands, more often than not being the first England player in position to collect a tactical kick from the opposition.

More importantly he was a demon tackler and could steal or deny possession, slowing down the opposition to the point of exasperation. Richards, England's most capped No 8 with 48 appearances, was, above all, a man to be relied on in a crisis.

Twin towers of the lineout Wade Dooley and Paul Ackford became a world-class second-row partnership for England, while captain Carling, far right, had blossomed into an outstanding centre

winger Rory Underwood, who skipped around several defenders from 22 metres out with less than 10 minutes remaining to score his 26th international try.

Teague crossed the line again with just moments left on the clock to make the win certain, while Hodgkinson's conversion and two penalties sent him to 46 points and past Dusty Hare's record total for England in the championship. And then came France, at Twickenham, and a thriller to

secure the Grand Slam. England saved their best for the last game, and overcame a French side full of flair and threatening enough to score a superb try that started from behind their own posts.

France may have outscored England by three tries to one, but it mattered not, they lost 21-19 and the Grand Slam was once again England's, only the country's third in 63 years.

History Makers

England's 1992 team was a strong one, and they knew it. Having
tasted in one season the high of a Grand Slam and then the low of
World Cup final defeat, Will Carling's men entered the
Five Nations on course to secure their place in history

England now carried with them an air of expectancy. By 1992, following their Grand Slam triumph of the year before, when they also made the World Cup final, this was an England team confident in their own strengths and their ability to achieve the first successive Five Nations cleansweeps for 58 years.

Only second-row stalwart Paul Ackford was missing from the 1991 squad, having chosen to retire, and England were in strong shape. The same could not be said of Scotland, England's first opponents at Murrayfield. They were very weak in the pack following the retirements of flankers Finlay Calder and John Jeffrey, although they did embarrass their opponents early on by scoring a pushover try.

But while England's pack did not dominate as it had done the previous year, the back line, employing new coach Dick Best's mantra of attacking at the right time, came to the fore. Winger Rory Underwood and recalled scrum half Dewi Morris ran in tries as England eventually cruised by Scotland 25-7, a score which flattered the home side.

The next hurdle was Ireland at Twickenham, an exhausting encounter for the players, but a successful one nonetheless. Full back Jonathan Webb was in inspiring form for the home side, and opened the scoring after a mere 23 seconds with a try straight from the kick-off.

He added another try, plus four conversions and two penalties, to finish the game with 22 points, equalling wing Douglas Lambert's 81-year-old record for an Englishman in the tournament. In all England ran in six tries and Ireland

You pass it, we'll kick it – many found England's forward-dominated style sterile, with the ball rarely getting beyond scrum half Dewi Morris, right, except when Jon Webb, below, or Rob Andrew, far right, kicked penalties. But by 1992 they had broken free and played a more expansive game

were ruthlessly dispatched 38-9. The French game in Paris matched England's controlled discipline with a France team who displayed a remarkable ability to self-destruct. A farcical collision between Alain Penaud and Jean-Luc Sadourny as they attempted a scissors move in the centres led to a breakaway England try, and then all hell was let loose.

Irish referee Stephen Hilditch had little option but to dismiss first Gregoire Lascube, for stamping, and then shortly afterwards Vincent Moscato, for head-butting, and France were left a beaten and confused rabble, eventually going down 31-13 thanks to tries by Morris and Webb, who was to set a new record of 67 points this campaign.

And so Wales came to Twickenham as the final hurdle between England and a second successive Grand Slam. But this was a weak Welsh side intent only on

"The players have been magnificent down the years, looking after me rather than me looking after them. The whole set-up is so much more relaxed these days simply because they are all so dedicated and so aware of getting in the right frame of mind. I think our victories in Paris have proved that."

ENGLAND CAPTAIN WILL CARLING on the secret to back-to-back Grand Slams

damage limitation. England produced an average performance from a side capable of much more, but three tries in a score of 24-0 meant a total of 15 in the tournament, and, more importantly, another Grand Slam. It was a fabulous achievement, Will

KEY PLAYER 1992

Brian Moore

Alan Jones, a former coach of Australia, called Brian Moore "the brains of the forwards, one of the great organisers in world rugby. He has made an extraordinary contribution to the England side."

Moore, off the field an articulate lawyer, was a fiery character on the pitch who went by the name of Pitbull. His England career spanned eight years and brought him 64 caps, a record for an England hooker. His qualities were many, from inspired pack leadership to some of the most precise lineout throwing the game has seen. In addition, Moore was ruthless, as hard as iron, and "would stand up to an approaching double-decker bus" in the words of second-rower Wade Dooley.

The added bonuses of Moore's game were his ball-handling skills and mobility, plus amazing stamina. His presence often meant England effectively had a four-man back row.

Quite possibly the outstanding player of one of England's most successful eras.

Carling's side becoming only the third team, after England in 1914 and 1924, in the history of the championship to achieve successive Grand Slams. But critics downplayed their success, saying England were like the big bully beating up little kids in the playground. But it was hardly England's fault that they were so good and the rest so poor.

A new Plan, a new Slam

England had a fresh coach in 1995 and a fresh approach. Gone were the days of forward-dominated, 10-man rugby, said Jack Rowell. And so they were, until that is Scotland needed beating for the Grand Slam

The 1995 season marked coach Jack Rowell's first foray into the Five Nations, and for it he wanted an England team prepared to play a more expansive game, a team who would score tries with backs and forwards integrating better in a 15-man game.

The first test of this new dynamic mindset came in Dublin against the Irish in a piercingly cold, howling gale. The game plan held together well, with tight control up front in the pack and then the centres, in particular a resurgent Will Carling, punching holes in the Irish defence. A 20-8 victory was well deserved and included three tries, one apiece for Carling, wing Tony Underwood and back-row member Ben Clarke.

When the French come to Twickenham it is one of the most eagerly awaited of international clashes. For 1995 in particular, the match had the makings of a tough encounter. France were jubilant after clinching their first series win over the All Blacks the summer before in New

Right, boys, hands on hips, left leg first, follow me – Rob Andrew, top, shows his leadership of the English back line, while Ben Clarke, right, and Tony Underwood, far right, make their marks

"There had been so much tension surrounding the Scotland fixture that there was more relief than pleasure in the dressing room after we had won, signalling our third Grand Slam in five years. It was an odd feeling. Rob Andrew said that the whole England camp was more tense than he'd seen it for a very long time."

FULL BACK MIKE CATT
on England's triumph

Zealand. But the English were unstoppable in front of their home crowd. Rowell called it a "storming performance" as his side ran in three tries – two for Underwood and one for Jeremy Guscott – and were never threatened in a 31-10 romp.

Against the Welsh in England's next match, Tony Underwood's esteemed brother Rory finally scored his first try at the Cardiff Arms Park, and added his second soon after, exorcising the awful memory of Ieuan Evans's try two years previously as the visitors played

out a comfortable 23-9 win. But in Paris on the same day, Scotland were causing the mightiest of upsets, beating France for the first time on French soil for 26 years, with full back and captain Gavin Hastings memorably breaking through on to Gregor Townsend's reverse pass to score a crucial try under the posts in a hard-fought 23-21 win.

That meant the two old enemies would, for the second time in six seasons, be playing off to decide who would claim the Grand Slam, and England had a score to settle after defeat

at Murrayfield in 1990. In front of their home crowd this time, England overcame a feisty Scottish side, but their hopes of playing an expansive game had to be put to one side.

Instead, England relied on the boot of fly half Rob Andrew, and he delivered in style. Seven successful penalty kicks and a drop goal gave Andrew all the English points in a 24-12 victory, equalling the record for an individual in the Five Nations. It was not a thrilling encounter, but it was enough to bring England another Grand Slam.

KEY PLAYER 1995

Will Carling

By the 1995 season Will Carling already had a place firmly etched in English rugby history, but his exploits kept adding more chapters to the story.

On the pitch through 1994, Carling had struggled to hit top form in an international shirt, and the appointment of Jack Rowell indicated that, while Carling would be first choice to lead the team, he had to prove he was worth his place as a player. This he did, and England were bolstered by his rock-solid tackling and barnstorming runs.

The '95 season was also something of a strange year for Carling off the pitch. After his infamous referral in a television documentary to the RFU committee as "57 old farts" unable to move the game into the professional era, his targets took their revenge by sacking Carling as England captain, and it took player power and overwhelming public support to have him reinstated for the World Cup campaign that summer.

Love him or loathe him, and there are plenty on either side of the fence, Carling's contribution to English rugby has been immense. Capped for the first time in 1988, and made captain later that year, he led England to three Grand Slams, a World Cup final in 1991 and a semi-final in 1995.

In all he led his country in 59 of his 72 internationals and his record of 44 wins, one draw and 14 defeats as skipper is unlikely to be beaten.

Full back Mike Catt, right, made his full Five Nations debut in 1995 and helped England to a Grand Slam

"In the previous seven years England had developed a style that was set-piece orientated and relatively static. It had been successful in the northern hemisphere, but by the time I became involved, midway through 1994, I felt England were running out of tries. With few immediate challenges to positions in the England team, I decided to hold the team stable and work on a change of style."

NEW COACH JACK ROWELL
explains his philosophy

Carling's Last Stand

England's 1996 Grand Slam campaign went no further than the first
hurdle in France, but the season which saw Carling stand down
as captain still brought the Five Nations title and a Triple Crown

The hopes for another back-to-back Grand Slam double were dashed by France in Paris in the opening encounter of the 1996 series, Thomas Castaignède's drop goal and impish tongue-poking celebration signalling a massive anti-climax for England's expectant fans.

With just two minutes left and the scores level at 12-12, the English still had a chance to extend their eight-year hold over France in the Five Nations, but the French centre kicked his side to glory and England into making plans for Triple Crown consolation.

Nevertheless, the English performance that day in Paris was heroic, particularly in defence. France were the better team but attacked only tentatively, and neither side managed to score a try. Back at Twickenham to entertain

Brothers Rory and Tony
Underwood first played
together for England in
1995, the same year
fly half Paul Grayson
made his debut

The centres of attention – Guscott, top, and Will Carling formed a magical midfield partnership for England in the 1990s

the Welsh, England again disappointed. Indeed, Wales took the lead early on thanks to some quick thinking at a penalty by fly half Arwel Thomas which resulted in a try in the corner for flanker Hemi Taylor.

England awoke from their slumbers, and although Paul Grayson at fly half did not have his most memorable game, tries either side of half-time by Rory Underwood and Jeremy Guscott put the English ahead, and there they stayed, running out 21-15 winners.

A month later and England travelled to Murrayfield, where the resurgent Scots awaited needing one more win to

secure an unexpected Grand Slam. Memories of 1990 were in the air and if the English wanted revenge, they would have been happy with the result, an 18-9 victory for the visitors.

It was mainly thanks to a powerful display by their forwards and, in particular, No 8 Dean Richards, surprisingly called up for his 47th cap. With England's front five dominant, Richards squeezed the life out of the game and Grayson kicked six penalties.

The Triple Crown could now be clinched with a win over the Irish at Twickenham, but the Five Nations title would not be England's unless Wales overcame the French, which amazingly they did, 16-15, in front of a jubilant Cardiff crowd. England duly beat Ireland 28-15 and, despite disappointing their fans throughout the campaign (the team scored only three tries in four games), the season was sweetened by the knowledge that they were still Europe's top team.

And the man who had done much to lead them there, Will Carling, relinquished his captaincy at the top, although limping off after 33 minutes of his last game in charge was probably not the farewell he had in mind.

> "It was a great way to finish and to have won the championship is unbelievable. You can't expect to run through people in international rugby, you have to move the opposition defence around and create a hole, and I think we played some great rugby."
>
> WILL CARLING
> on his last season as captain

Rory Underwood

The 1996 season will not go down as a vintage one for England's flying winger Rory Underwood – his country's style of play in a Triple Crown season did not allow his talents to be shown to the full – but that cannot disguise the fact that since making his international debut in 1984, Underwood's contribution to England's success has been huge.

Underwood actually retired in 1992, but found the pull of international rugby too great and returned later that same year to team up in the England side with his younger brother Tony on the opposite wing.

While his defence was sometimes unfairly criticised, Underwood's greatest attribute, his lightning pace, could not be faulted and throughout a career which garnered 85 caps, the most by any English player, his speed on the wing helped him to 49 tries, another England record.

He also equalled the mark for the most tries scored in a single match for England by running in five against Fiji in 1989.

Without doubt Underwood was a true great in English and world rugby history.

FFR

france

Gallic style, champagne rugby and an occasionally chaotic approach to discipline – after a shaky start to the Five Nations the French created a glorious legend which they have lived up to ever since

We're No 1 – the French team celebrate claiming their first back-to-back Grand Slams in 1998. True to their unpredictable nature they finished bottom the next season

FFR

BY
JEAN-PIERRE RIVES

'The Five Nations is a dream, an atmosphere…'

Jean-Pierre Rives was a ferocious competitor on the rugby field – and a charming, generous opponent off it. France's most-capped flanker, his face frequently lined with blood, the 'Blond Bombshell' captained his country a record 34 times and took them to Grand Slam glory in 1981. When asked for his thoughts on the Five Nations, he declined to write "all that boring stuff about who scored a try in what game", explaining: "The Five Nations is a dream, an atmosphere." He is now an abstract painter and sculptor – and, it appears, a poet. Merci beaucoup, Jean-Pierre…

Disbelief both blue and white as France claim victory at Twickenham in 1997 on their way to the Grand Slam

Le Tournoi des Cinq Nations,
c'est Hélène de Troie;
c'est Léonidas aux Thermopyles;
c'est un enfant qui rit,
c'est aussi quelquefois des hommes qui pleurent.
Participer au Tournoi,
c'est pénétrer dans une autre dimension…
à partir de ce point-là,
votre ticket n'est plus valable.
Le Tournoi, c'est l'émotion;
c'est une belle jeune fille en robe de dentelle;
c'est le garde barrière de Saint-Simon,
il porte un grand chapeau blanc
et parle d'exotisme à son perroquet…
Le Tournoi, c'est un rêve d'enfant et tout,
autour, sent le camphre,
l'amour et l'aventure humaine.

The Five Nations Championship,
it is Helen of Troy;
it is Leonidas at Thermopylae;
it is a child who laughs,
but also sometimes men who cry.
To take part in the Five Nations
is to enter another dimension…
beyond that point,
your ticket is no longer valid.
The Five Nations, it is emotion;
it is a beautiful girl in a lace dress;
it is the signalman at Saint-Simon,
who wears a big white hat
and speaks of exotic places to his parrot…
The Five Nations, it is a child's dream,
and everything, all around, smells of camphor,
of love and of human adventure.

Notes:
• HELEN OF TROY, in Greek legend, was the most beautiful woman in the world. According to Homer's *Iliad*, she was the wife of Menelaus, king of Sparta. Aphrodite, the goddess of love, helped Paris, a prince of Troy, to abduct her. Agamemnon, the brother of Menelaus, set out to rescue Helen with 1,000 ships (hence the saying that she had 'the face that launched 1,000 ships'). This started the Trojan War, in which the Greeks captured Troy using the Trojan Horse.
• LEONIDAS was the warrior king of Sparta who, during the Persian War of the 5th century BC, tried to stop King Xerxes of Persia marching on Greece. Leonidas and his 300 Spartans bravely defended a narrow mountain pass until they were all killed. Leonidas is also Jean-Pierre's favourite Belgian chocolate.
• SAINT-SIMON, says Jean-Pierre, is a small, nondescript town. He suggests you could substitute Reading or Crewe. While the signalman waves off the trains on journeys to faraway places, he must remain at home in Saint-Simon, where the only one who listens to his dreams of escape is his parrot.

Jean-Pierre Rives,
poetry in motion

PIERRE VILLEPREUX'S ALL-TIME FRANCE FIVE NATIONS XV

Pierre Villepreux played 34 times for France between 1967 and 1972, including 18 Five Nations matches in a six-year period when the French won the title three times. The former full back is now a world-renowned coach who guided his country to back-to-back Grand Slams. He has been admired and abused in equal measure for his devotion to running rugby, so it is no surprise to find his dream team packed with enough attacking class to set the pitch ablaze

1 Patou Paparemborde
(Loosehead prop)
Not only very good in the scrum but also a great player of the ball. Ahead of his time, the forerunner of the modern-day prop.

Captain and hooker Daniel Dubroca, above right, and Serge Blanco, right, often rescued France with the sheer force of their personalities

2 Daniel Dubroca (Hooker)
An extremely dynamic player, as much in defence as in attack, who knew exactly how to inspire confidence in his fellow players, especially those in the front row.

3 Gerard Cholley (Tighthead prop)
Physically very strong, a player who knew how to exploit his height and weight to the full, in the ruck and maul as well as in the scrum.

4 Benoit Dauga (Lock)
An outstanding taker of the ball, Benoit knew how to do everything with it. His capacity for anticipating the play of the backs meant that he could contribute to the game across a wide range of situations, not just in the lineout and the scrum.

5 Claude Spanghero (Lock)
Like Benoit, he combined superb running ability with technical expertise, playing with flair and imagination. He was a forward with the qualities of a back.

6 Jean-Pierre Rives (Flanker)
Captain
A great captain who led by example even in the most difficult of circumstances. An outstanding defender whose ability to regain possession from rucks and mauls was second to none.

7 Jean-Claude Skrela (Flanker)
Complemented Jean-Pierre Rives perfectly. Undoubtedly a first-class attacking runner, but he also showed remarkable tenacity when pursuing the ball carrier.

His vision of the game was absolutely perfect and his passing was recognised by all the world's experts as being outstanding.

11 Patrice Lagisquet (Wing)
A superb finisher thanks to his speed and a very talented player not only in his own position on the wing but one who could provide exceptional support through knowing how to make himself available.

12 Philippe Sella (Centre)
The most-capped player in French rugby, a player of class and courage who never missed an opportunity to run with the ball. Not only quick, but he also knew how to use his power as effectively in defence as in attack.

13 Didier Codorniou (Centre)
'Le Petit Prince' of French rugby who played his rugby like a great pianist,

with precision and flair. His ability to do the 'right thing at the right moment' compensated for any lack of size. His defensive play was as intelligent as his attacking, allowing him to cope with any situation.

14 Philippe Saint-André (Wing)
A fast and powerful player, whose most outstanding attribute was his capacity to intervene anywhere on the pitch. Thanks to his power he had a great ability to retain the ball and score by forcing himself over the try line. In addition, he was a great captain.

15 Serge Blanco (Full back)
The most celebrated of all, he initiated the most daring and sometimes the craziest of moves. But his daring allowed him to score many, many tries and, above all, to rescue France when all seemed lost.

Record breakers – Sella, left, and Rives, above, are the most capped French players in their positions of centre and flanker

8 Walter Spanghero (No 8)
A great all-rounder, Walter could play in every forward position except hooker. His great hands allowed him to develop technical skills not commonly found among forwards.

9 Richard Astre (Scrum half)
A player of great class, the intelligence of his play and his sense of strategy meant that he could guide and direct his fellow players through the quality of his decision making.

10 Jo Maso (Fly half)
Centre or No 10, Jo was one of the most talented players in French rugby.

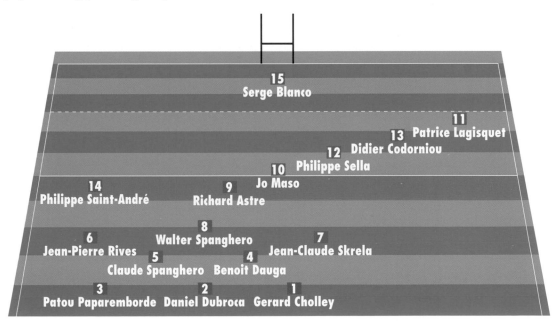

FFR

four Become five

The International Championship turned into the Five Nations with
the inclusion of France in 1910, but it would be a long time before
Gallic flair made much impact on their European brothers

The French international rugby team made their debut in the new Five Nations tournament on January 1, 1910, at Swansea against Wales, who happened to be the last winners of the International Championship.

The outcome was predictable. Wales tore France apart, running in 10 tries in a 49-14 win. In fact, France went on to finish their first championship season on the end of a whitewash, something they suffered again in 1912, 1913 and 1914. The first French victory came against Scotland in Paris in 1911, 16-15, but between 1910 and 1929 France registered a mere seven championship wins.

Between 1932 and 1939, France were excluded from the tournament because French clubs were paying their players to play. The French Federation was given the ultimatum during the 1931 Five Nations that unless amateurism was restored, punitive action would be taken. Failure to act excluded France from the championship until play resumed after the Second World War in 1947.

The 1950s

Slowly French rugby began to rise towards greater heights. In 1951 the country scored their first ever victory in England. On a soggy day in February, the French laid their Twickenham bogey to rest, with flanker Jean Prat particularly outstanding in an 11-3 win in which he scored a try, a conversion and a drop goal.

France registered three wins in a season for the first time that year, and finished runners-up to Ireland, the only side to beat them in the campaign. In 1954 France repeated

their three-win season, losing only to Wales, but more importantly grabbed a share of the championship, finishing in a three-way tie with Wales and England.

Another share of the title was secured in 1955 thanks to victories against Scotland (15-0), Ireland (5-3) and England (16-9). It was only again the Welsh who beat France, 16-11 in Paris, a disappointment for the home side as it denied the country their first ever Grand Slam. Instead they were in a two-way tie with Wales.

1959 – Champions at last

France's first outright championship title finally came in 1959, and was built on the strength and versatility of the team's forwards.

The French pack proved itself adept at attacking rugby. It was a mobile set of forwards capable of neat interplay while keeping the ball alive, as well as being able to launch dangerous onslaughts from the set piece.

Scotland succumbed first to the powerful French, beaten in Paris 9-0, but a 3-3 draw against England at Twickenham threatened to stall France's momentum. However, a barnstorming performance in front of a home crowd of 55,000 against Wales, when sunny conditions proved ideal for France's fast, mobile rugby, brought an 11-4 victory, and with it the country's first Five Nations title.

The fact that Ireland beat the French in the final game of the season, 9-5 at Lansdowne Road, was an irrelevance – France's unique blend of champagne rugby had arrived in the championship at last.

*The Cockerel in flight –
wins over Scotland,
above, and Wales,
right, gave France their
first title in 1959*

FFR

Jean Prat

A stalwart of the French team between 1945 and 1952 – a period during which he missed only one international game – Jean Prat was already a key figure in French rugby history before he was elevated to the captaincy in 1953.

The Lourdes flanker had played a role in France's first win in Wales (in 1948), he had been instrumental in France's first victory at Twickenham (in 1951), and he also had a hand in the first defeat of Scotland by France on Scottish soil (in 1952).

As skipper, though, Prat was able to lead his country to new heights. He was a strong captain and, although his 1954 team were inexperienced (seven members of the side which took the field for the opening game against Scotland had three caps or fewer), they were well drilled and had a good strategy.

Good enough to bring a share of the championship, at least, with Prat grabbing an important drop goal in the vital clash with England that ensured a share of the title.

His leadership qualities were still in evidence in 1955 when he again guided his country to a shared Five Nations title and, indeed, to within an ace of a first Grand Slam.

It was not to be, defeat against Wales denying Prat a taste of overall triumph, but he retired after the 1955 campaign with legendary status in French rugby, as well as world records in drop goals and conversions for an international forward.

Allez, La France

France's first outright championship title galvanised the country into a stunning run of success. The early 1960s belonged to the French and before the decade was out, they were able to celebrate their first Grand Slam

In the 1960s France had an attacking style, below against Ireland and right against Wales, and flanker Michel Crauste, top, was one of those to benefit with the first hat-trick by a forward

1960 – Champions

France picked up where they had left off a year previously, bringing a form of attacking, free-flowing rugby to the Five Nations which almost swept all before it. The French had an appetite for tries which was irrepressible, and through the campaign they ran in 11, their best performance so far in the championship and a mark which would not be exceeded until 1976 when they scored 13.

Scotland were beaten 13-11 at Murrayfield, Wales 16-8 at Cardiff and Ireland crushed 23-6 in Paris. Only England showed resistance in defence to the French attacking manoeuvres, and their 3-3 draw at Stade Colombes was well earned, also ensuring that the championship was shared between England and France.

1961 – Champions

France once again took the championship outright in 1961, although their first Grand Slam still remained elusive. In a bizarre repeat of the previous season, it was again only England who gained any result against the French. The venue this time was Twickenham, but the result was again a draw, 5-5, each side scoring a converted try.

Scotland succumbed 11-0 in Paris and Ireland fell in Dublin 15-3. The Welsh took pride from their performance in Paris, making seven changes in the pack but still running France close to lose 8-6, their fourth successive defeat by the French.

In this campaign England were only able to add a win and two defeats to the draw against the French, so Les Bleus could celebrate their second outright Five Nations title even before the team's final game against Ireland.

1962 – Champions

A fourth successive championship victory, and the third outright in four years, came in 1962 courtesy of three wins and one defeat, by Wales 3-0 in Cardiff. It was the first time any nation had won or shared the Five Nations in four successive years.

At times in 1962 France were quite superb, particularly in the 13-0 demolition of England in Paris, France's best win against the English in the championship for 14 years,

Beret, beret strange

André Behoteguy, who, with his brother Henri, was a regular member of the French threequarter line in the 1920s, always wore a beret when he played.

with flanker Michel Crauste making history by becoming the first forward to score a hat-trick of tries in the Five Nations. At other times in 1962 the French stuttered to display individual moments of brilliance rather than outright domination, for example, against Ireland in Paris where the 11-0 scoreline belied the effort of the Irish. But France were undoubtedly setting the standard for others to chase.

> "Where more brilliant French sides have failed, the French of 1968 have succeeded at last in the clean sweep and there is nothing like a match at Cardiff Arms Park to end a drought."
>
> MICHAEL MELFORD
> The Daily Telegraph

1967 – Champions

The season started badly for France in 1967, with a 9-8 defeat at home against Scotland, but it rapidly improved and culminated in another championship win.

Guy Cambérabéro was an inspiration, proving deadly accurate with his kicking off the ground and out of hand. The fly half, who, with his brother Lilian, scored all France's points in a 20-14 victory over Australia that year, notched a French record of 32 points for the season as his country put the early reversal against Scotland behind them and rattled off three convincing victories.

1968 - The Grand Slam

The long wait for a French Grand Slam was finally ended on a wet, muddy day at Cardiff Arms Park 58 years after France first entered the championship when they overcame a 9-3 half-time deficit against Wales to run out 14-9 winners and claim their clean sweep of victories.

With the Cambérabéro brothers usually favouring the kick rather than the pass, this was not the most exciting or adventurous of French teams – the championship-winning sides of 1959 through to 1962 had shown more flair and style.

But the 1968 team led by Christian Carrère were efficient and ruthless in exploiting opportunities and grinding the opposition down.

The winning sequence started at Murrayfield where Scotland were beaten 8-6. Then Ireland were defeated 16-6 in Paris, England also lost in France, 14-9, and finally, Wales were beaten on the hallowed turf of the Arms Park.

It may not have been vintage rugby by the French, but it at last had that special Grand Slam bouquet.

KEY PLAYER 1960

Christian Carrère

Flanker Christian Carrère won his first cap for France in 1966 at the age of 23. Just two years later he was made captain of the side which would go on to land France's first Grand Slam.

It speaks volumes for the leadership talents of the young man from Toulon that he was able to take the helm of a side who were not as talented as previous French teams and mould them into a dominant force. This despite the numerous changes the selectors made through the course of the '68 championship.

Carrère's method of captaincy was calm and collected, but he commanded total respect.

The season following the Grand Slam was marred by injury and Carrère played only two Five Nations games, but he resumed the captaincy in 1970 when France played some inspired rugby, thrashing England by a record 35-13, and again won a share of the championship, only being denied a second Grand Slam by defeat in Wales.

Carrère finished his career in 1971 with only 27 caps to his name – but his exploits ensured a special place in French rugby history.

A Second Triumph

Following the heady heights of French success in the 1960s,
the next decade proved almost barren by comparison. Almost, but
not quite, as there was still another Grand Slam to celebrate

rance started the 1970s where they had spent most of the preceding decade – on top of the Five Nations. The 1970 championship was not a classic, but France, along with the other successful nation of the 1960s, Wales, were the team to beat.

Wales actually defeated France in the 1970 campaign, 11-6 in Cardiff, but the Welsh also managed to lose 14-0 in Ireland, so both sides finished the season with three wins apiece to share the championship title. The highlight of the season for France was the crushing defeat of England in Paris by 35-13. It was the first time any nation had scored that many points against the English, and the cornerstone of the win was the performance of the French forwards – led again by Christian Carrère – who dominated the setpiece and proved too powerful in the loose.

1977 – Grand Slam

Compared with the attacking rugby which had characterised most French success in previous championship seasons, the Grand Slam won in 1977 was not the most stylish. France used their big, heavy guns in the pack to pulverise the opposition into submission, and relied on a watertight defence more than a free-flowing attack to gain victory over the other four nations.

The French went through the 1977 Five Nations without conceding a try, something the country had done only once before, during the championship-winning season of

France beat Ireland in Paris on the way to winning the 1970 Five Nations title, which was shared with Wales, opposite

"The French on their day play rugby football with a mastery and a brilliance all of their own – and yesterday was their day."
MICHAEL MELFORD, THE DAILY TELEGRAPH after France crushed England in 1970

FFR

KEY PLAYER 1977

Jacques Fouroux

The 1977 Grand Slam was the Five Nations swansong for France's scrum half and captain, Jacques Fouroux. His retirement was controversial – a severe dislike of French selector Ellie Pebeyre and a loss of patience with media criticism led him to quit.

Fouroux's technical attributes as a scrum half may have had equal in French rugby, but his leadership skills were without parallel.

In 21 games as the captain of France, his team lost only seven. The fact he played only 27 internationals seems a strange injustice, but, for reasons best known to themselves, his style was not fully appreciated by the authorities.

Le Petit Général, whose shrewd tactical acumen led France to only their second Grand Slam in the 67 years since the country joined the Five Nations, deserved better.

1962. First in their series of matches were Wales, the defending Grand Slam champions. The Welsh were to outscore France 66 points to 58 on their way to the runners-up spot this season – but, in Paris, France ground them down slowly and ran out 16-9 winners to put their campaign on track.

Then came a mighty clash against England at Twickenham where the French defence in general, and their forwards in particular, refused to yield. There was an incredible atmosphere, with England's headquarters a cauldron of partisan support which left the visitors with their backs against the wall even before kick-off.

And, during the game, things hardly improved. Refereeing decisions went against the French, with the flurry of penalties awarded in England's favour forcing captain and scrum half Jacques Fouroux to use all his skills of diplomacy to keep his team disciplined and focused.

France did gain help from an unexpected source, however, English full back Alastair Hignell having the kind of game he will wish to forget. His goal-kicking fell apart as he missed five out of six penalty attempts, but, even more crucially, he also spilled a high ball in defence which led to France's solitary score, a try by Francois Sangalli. That was enough to bring a 4-3 victory, and keep the Grand Slam dream alive.

The next game, against Scotland in Paris, was a complete contrast to the match with England. France played some exquisite rugby en route to winning 23-3, with two of the tries registered by front row players, Alain Paco and Robert Paparemborde.

Which just left Ireland, in Dublin, and the French half back pairing of Fouroux and Jean-Pierre Romeu weaved a magic spell around the Irish which produced a 15-6 victory for the French, and the country's second Grand Slam crown.

The Rives Musketeers

The charismatic flanker and captain, his blond locks
marking him as a beacon of the national side, led France to
a third Grand Slam with a powerful display at Twickenham

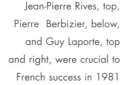

Jean-Pierre Rives, top,
Pierre Berbizier, below,
and Guy Laporte, top
and right, were crucial to
French success in 1981

Bill Beaumont's England side had swept all before them in the 1980 Five Nations on the way to the Grand Slam, while France had experienced a dismal season, managing only one win. So only the foolish or the madly Gallic expected the Cockerel to crow in 1981.

However, it was a reconstructed French team who took to the field for the opening game against Scotland in Paris, including at least two men new to the Five Nations but destined to add in style to its glorious history, Serge Blanco and Pierre Berbizier. In addition, the side were captained by Jean-Pierre Rives and coached by Jacques Fouroux, both veterans of the Grand Slam-winning side of 1977.

Fouroux, renowned for his mantra of favouring three tactics in international rugby: possession, possession and possession, assembled a side around a big set of forwards but with a mobile and talented back row spearheaded by Rives.

The result was not the prettiest rugby France have ever played, but it was effective and also defensively mean, and Scotland were beaten 16-9, Blanco scoring the first try of his Five Nations career. On the same day England, somewhat surprisingly, lost 21-19 to Wales at Cardiff Arms Park, English full back Dusty Hare missing a penalty in the last minute.

These results opened the door for Fouroux's side, and a victory in Dublin against the Irish, 19-13, took them a step closer to the clean sweep. Guy Laporte at fly half was the killer of Ireland's hopes. Making his international debut at the age of 28, Laporte scored two long-range drop goals and a brace of penalties to seal a good day's work.

Wales got a lively reception in Paris for the next game of the series, and it proved to be a real battle. Once again France had to rely on the kicking skills of Laporte, and his three successful penalty kicks made all the difference as France emerged on top 19-15.

That meant victory over England would secure a Grand Slam, but also that the English could redeem their season with a win for a share of the championship. Conditions at Twickenham on the day were not conducive to a free-spirited game of rugby – a gale was blowing down the

Jean-Pierre Rives

The sight of Jean-Pierre Rives in full flight off the back of a set piece, long, blond hair flowing, was inspiring. His pace and vision as a flanker were without equal, and his tackling was robust.

Rives announced himself to the world of international rugby in 1975, stamping his authority on an English side playing in front of their home crowd. He played in all Five Nations games between 1976 and 1978, including in Jacques Fouroux's Grand Slam-winning side in 1977.

When Rives was elevated to the position of captain in 1979, he set about rediscovering a more liberal approach to the game in the mould of French sides of the past, an approach ditched in favour of thundering forward play in the late 1970s.

This style brought France's first win in New Zealand, but a struggle in the 1980 Five Nations.

Under the coaching of Fouroux in '81, Rives' side adapted to combine powerful forwards with stylish backs, linked by a superb back row including the captain. That brought a Grand Slam, and Rives nearly led his side to another in 1984.

long way out to open the scoring and then Rives fed his fellow back-row member Pierre Lacans near the corner for a try.

The possession had been won by the French from a quick lineout taken near the English 22-metre line, but Berbizier, who took the throw-in, had used the wrong ball and the score should not have been allowed by Scottish referee Allan Hosie.

No matter. Laporte kicked the conversion and just before the break Rives again played the link man to set winger Laurent Pardo on his way to score. Just for good measure, Laporte registered another drop goal just before the whistle for half-time.

England could not match the effectiveness of the French when they had use of the wind in the second half and struggled to get a grip on the game, despite Maurice Colclough working miracles in the English lineout and Beaumont, his second-row colleague, again in barnstorming form.

England's full back Marcus Rose landed four penalty goals to edge his side closer to the French, but the home side could not do enough and the final score of 16-12 gave France their third Grand Slam.

length of the pitch – but both sides were already reliant on their packs doing the bulk of the work.

It proved to be a titanic struggle, and not without controversy. The French took advantage of the wind at their backs in the first half and built a 16-0 advantage by the break. Laporte again dropped a goal from a

Eighties Men

With the Grand Slam triumph of 1981 as a springboard,
France fashioned a team who went on to be the dominant force
of the decade and sealed another Grand Slam in 1987

The 1980s undoubtedly belonged to France. The Grand Slam of 1981 under the leadership of Jean-Pierre Rives was followed up by relentless success throughout the decade. In 1983 France shared the Five Nations title with Ireland, and two second places were then followed in 1986 by another shared title, this time with Scotland.

It was the first of four straight seasons in which the French finished outright or joint leaders in the championship, matching their triumphant run of the early 1960s. A share of the title with Wales came in 1988 and the next season, France, quite fittingly, ended the decade by winning the Five Nations outright, the ninth occasion they had achieved such a feat.

And yet, sandwiched in between these successful years was an even more glorious campaign when France registered their fourth Grand Slam in 1987. Having beaten Wales 16-9 in Paris, the French team travelled to Twickenham to take on an English side which had already been well beaten by Ireland (17-0) and looked in disarray. Few expected France to lose at England's HQ, and many believed it would be a massacre.

France, indeed, did not lose, but it was far from the crushing victory that had been anticipated. The visitors, in fact, fell behind, thanks to three penalties from full back Marcus Rose. Unfortunately for England, the second half was dominated by the French. First a scissors move in the backs created the space for flanker Eric Champ, in outstanding form, to punch a huge hole in the English defence and slip a scoring pass to winger Eric Bonneval,

who crossed the line near the posts. With the scores level at 12-12 in the 64th minute, England's captain Richard Hill threw a risky pass to his half back partner Rob Andrew, some 30 metres from the French goal line.

The ball never reached Andrew. Instead it was plucked out of the air by Philippe Sella, who set off on a weaving 65-metre run which included two breathtaking feints to leave defenders Rose and Mike Harrison clutching air. The inevitable try set up victory, which ultimately came 19-15.

Scotland in Paris provided sturdy opposition in a classic encounter at Parc des Princes. The Scottish forwards were magnificent on the day, and if justice had been done, the

> **"It was an honourable day for Scotland, for France, and for rugby; honourable and hard."**
> CAPTAIN DANIEL DUBROCA
> after a close-fought win against Scotland set up the chance of the Grand Slam

Flanker Eric Champ, top, and wing Eric Bonneval, opposite, were prolific try-scorers in the exciting French team of Daniel Dubroca, right

Scots should have gone home rejoicing. The French played thoughtful rugby for the first 50 minutes, and attacked effectively. Bonneval was the principal thorn in Scottish sides, scoring three tries from the wing, and with 30 minutes to go France appeared to be home and dry, leading 22-7.

The Scots, though, led by the canny attacking of Roy Laidlaw and John Rutherford at half back, gave the French players and spectators the fright of their lives. Scotland came within a whisker of turning the deficit over completely and they could count themselves unlucky to lose 28-22 so good were they in the last half-hour.

Perhaps inspired by the way Scotland took the game to France in Paris, the Irish opened the match which could give France the Grand

Slam in flying fashion, and within 13 minutes had forged a 10-0 lead thanks to tries from Trevor Ringland and Michael Bradley.

This stung France into life, and although the Irish, on the back foot for the rest of the game, produced a heroic rearguard action, it was not enough. The French used the lineout to set up countless attacks and Champ rounded off a superb season with a brace of tries which sealed victory 19-13 and the Grand Slam.

The French side of 1987 went on to prove how good they were by prospering in the inaugural World Cup in Australasia in the summer. They reached the final with victory over Australia in a classic semi-final and only stumbled at that last hurdle, losing 29-9 to the mighty All Blacks.

> "Twenty, ten, even two years ago, such resolution and such good old British phlegm would have been unthinkable from the French. They would have lost their temper with referee Clive Norling, they would have blown a fuse and blown the match with it. But not now."
>
> JOHN REASON, THE DAILY TELEGRAPH
> on France's new-found discipline

Serge Blanco

Full back Serge Blanco played in two French Grand Slam sides and he was a major influence in France's domination of the 1980s.

His made his debut at the start of the decade and by the time he retired in 1992 he had accumulated 93 caps and scored 233 points for his country, including 38 tries.

Blanco played rugby with abandon and enjoyment. Unpredictable and elusive, he was capable of turning the direst position in defence into one of exciting counterattack with his silky running, as he did at Twickenham in 1991 from behind his own goal line when France scored one of the Five Nations' greatest tries.

There were few finer sights in the 1980s than Blanco appearing at speed in France's exciting threequarter line, and in the 1987 season he was at his best. His performance in the World Cup semi-final against Australia will live long in the memory, his last-gasp try in the corner to bring victory sealing a superb display.

Brand New Champions

France became the first country to have their name engraved
on the new Five Nations Trophy. But for a couple of cruel
bounces they could have been lifting it as Grand Slam champions

Troubled by home Test defeats against South Africa and, for the first time ever, Argentina, France entered the 1993 Five Nations under a cloud. When they began their campaign at Twickenham against an England team looking for their sixth successive win over their Continental cousins and a third consecutive Grand Slam, the omens were not good.

They were even worse after a tensely-fought 16-15 defeat by the English, whose previously successful gameplan of keeping the ball in the forwards and rumbling upfield had been stifled by the game's new laws. It was a defeat especially hard to take given two cruel interventions

Cambérabéro, below, and Lacroix, far right, two powerful threequarters who were prolific kickers

by the woodwork. The French made the early running, winger Philippe Saint-André the grateful recipient of some superb tactical kicking from fly half Didier Cambérabéro which had England full back Jon Webb in confusion and led to two tries in the first 16 minutes.

Then came the first piece of bad luck for the visiting side. A penalty attempt by Webb shortly before half-time rebounded off a post and straight into the arms of winger Ian Hunter, who gratefully plunged over the line. Against the run of play, England now held a 13-12 half-time lead.

Webb and Cambérabéro exchanged penalties in the second half to leave France trailing 16-15. And then came the second bad bounce. Drop goal attempts with minutes left by Cambérabéro and scrum half Aubin Hueber hit the crossbar and fell back into play. England held on for victory.

However, all was not lost. While England went on to crash in Cardiff 10-9 and see their hopes of another Grand Slam destroyed, France entertained Scotland in Paris, a city in which the Scots had not won since 1969. Indeed, they had never won at Parc des Princes. In truth, that losing streak should have ended in this match, but the normally reliable Gavin Hastings missed five out of his six penalty kicks at goal, and sloppy handling put paid to several scoring opportunities in open play.

Two penalties from Cambérabéro and a try from Thierry Lacroix, playing in the centres with Philippe Sella, were enough to see the French back to winning ways 11-3.

In Dublin against a spirited Irish team, France cruised home 21-6, scoring two tries through the backs – one for

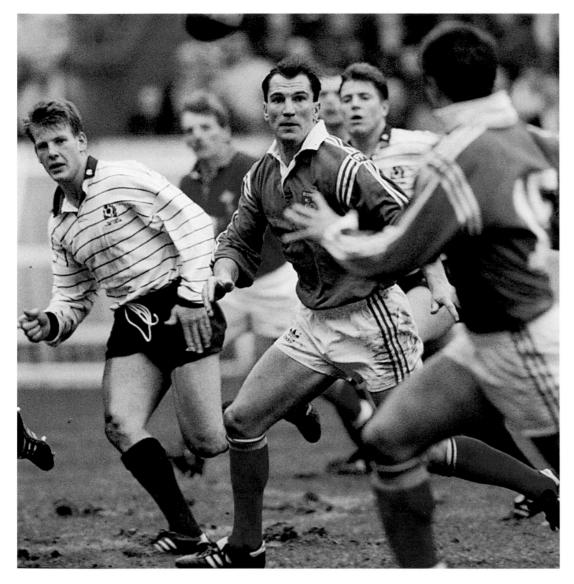

KEY PLAYER 1993

Philippe Sella

It is difficult to overestimate the exploits of Philippe Sella, a true rugby great, and his contribution to the game in France and across the world.

In attack from his position at centre, Sella was a genius – fast, creative, balanced and visionary. He seemed capable of squeezing through a gap which few other players would have even seen.

And in defence he could stop a flourishing attack with a single thundering tackle, a testimony to his superb positional play and reading of the game.

Sella came into the French national team in 1982 and was an integral part of the country's heady success of that decade. That he was still a key member of the threequarter line by the 1995 season, his last for France, is a measure of his worth.

In all, Sella collected 111 caps for his country, and scored 30 tries. He succeeded Serge Blanco as captain of France in 1991 and although his reign as the leader was not entirely successful, it can take nothing away from his reputation as one of the finest all-round centres of all time.

Saint-André and another for Sella, both coming in the last 10 minutes – and were never seriously threatened by an Irish team who would later do them a huge favour.

France wrapped up their season at the Parc des Princes against Wales and even though the Welsh defence, in particular Scott Gibbs in the centre, was resolute, the French still managed to pull clear. Two tries from flanker Philippe Benetton sandwiched around one from Jean-Baptiste Lafond made for a healthy 26-10 victory.

At the same time over in Dublin, a resurgent Irish team, spurred on by the accurate boot of fly half Eric Elwood in his debut season, defeated England 17-3. It was a shock result which handed the new Five Nations Trophy to France without the need for another of that season's innovations, points difference.

FFR

High Five

France could only watch while England ruled the early 1990s, but
it was not long before a reshaped side sounded out their own claim
to be the team of the decade with a masterful fifth Grand Slam

> **"The gameplan
> I am aiming
> at is extremely
> ambitious. It is
> one which I
> believe corresponds
> perfectly with
> the French
> temperament.
> The important
> thing is that the
> players have the
> desire and
> intention to
> attack."**
> PIERRE VILLEPREUX
> signals France's return
> to running rugby

Up in arms – scrum half
Philippe Carbonneau,
right, and wing David
Venditti, far right, gave
France plenty of reasons
to celebrate in 1997

By the start of the 1997 Five Nations France were
undergoing hasty and necessary rebuilding after a
mauling in front of their home fans by the touring
South Africans. The selectors turned to a man billed as "the
prophet of running rugby", Pierre Villepreux, to instil some
of that old Gallic flair into the back division. Although
Villepreux enjoyed a high regard as a coach around the
world, he had been almost ignored by his home country's
national team since
retiring from Test rugby
in 1972.

> **"In the end at Twickenham,
> unlike at Waterloo, it was
> France who pounded
> longest – and hardest – as
> they lowered England's
> colours to bring the chariot
> to a shuddering halt."**
> THE SUNDAY TIMES
> on England's late breakdown

Pierre Villepreux was
brought in as assistant
to coach Jean-Claude
Skrela, and they aimed
to restore discipline,
rediscover team spirit,
and revive the inventive-
ness and fluidity which
had been the hallmark of
French teams of the past.
Despite injuries forcing unexpected changes in personnel,
under the combined gaze of Skrela and Villepreux, France
rose up to conquer all.

What was to be the fifth French Grand Slam campaign
started at Lansdowne Road against an Irish side which once
again performed heroics, but once again was found
wanting. The 32-15 victory was flattering to the visitors, but
it extended France's run of Five Nations victories over
Ireland to 12. The scourge of the Irish was French winger

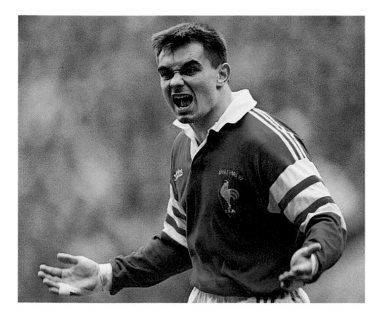

David Venditti, who grabbed a trio of tries, the second of which, on the hour, silenced the partisan crowd who were dreaming of greater things as their team hung on to an unlikely 15-12 lead. Venditti's third try, in injury time, simply confirmed Ireland's lack of stamina and concentration.

When France beat Wales 27-22 in Paris in their second match of the championship, the signs were obvious that the next game, against England, would be the crunch. The English had been in supreme form in their first two games, crushing Scotland 41-13 and Ireland 46-6 in Dublin.

The France-Wales match in Paris, meanwhile, was a classic. Skrela and Villepreux were

> "What we are very pleased about, more pleased than anything else, is that we won the match playing a style of rugby that we can all be proud of, with good team spirit that we had hoped would come together this season."
>
> PIERRE VILLEPREUX
> revels in the Grand Slam triumph after France beat Scotland

forced to field a much changed side because of injuries, particularly in the back division, but, at times, they still looked like world beaters.

France held a 20-10 lead at half-time but the Welsh fought back to within three points before eventually succumbing by five.

So to Twickenham, and the clash of the giants. And with the game two-thirds over, England had the French cold. A 20-6 lead had been established thanks to the boot of Paul Grayson and a try by Lawrence Dallaglio. The English pack was in control and thoughts of a French Grand Slam were on the ebb. Then, from the 61st minute, the game was turned on its head.

Winger Laurent Leflamand scored from a chip and chase and eight minutes later another try by the brilliant centre Christophe Lamaison, and his second successful conversion, brought the scores level at 20-20. A Lamaison penalty after 77 minutes sealed an extraordinary 23-20 French win.

On the last weekend of the championship, while England claimed the Triple Crown by beating Wales in Cardiff 34-13, France entertained Scotland with the Grand Slam in sight. The result was never in doubt, despite a Scottish rally in the second half, and France ran out glorious winners 47-20, serving up a wonderful feast of rugby for the home crowd, who gave their heroes a standing ovation which lasted well over 10 minutes after the final whistle.

The trademark champagne rugby of the French had been truly restored, and the Grand Slam prize was the very least it deserved, whatever England's supporters had to say.

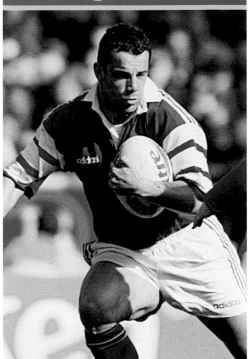

Christophe Lamaison

The Brive centre Christophe Lamaison was singled out by many as the crucial man in France's Grand Slam of 1997. In his first international season, Lamaison's place kicking was vital, particularly the four successful attempts out of five against England, including the late, winning penalty.

Lamaison ended the campaign with 42 points in all, 37 of them from the boot. And of the 15 kicks he attempted at goal throughout the series, he missed only two.

But there was more to Lamaison's game than his kicking. He was a pivotal force in the centre, with pace aplenty and the necessary vision to open up defences with France's attacking back line.

Appearing almost from nowhere, in 1997 Lamaison was, quite simply, a revelation.

FFR

A french Toast

Inspired by the bottle blond Castaignède, France uncorked a special vintage in 1998, becoming only the second country in the history of the Five Nations to secure back-to-back Grand Slams

The prospects of France successfully defending their Grand Slam title looked none too bright at the beginning of the 1998 Five Nations. Just as they had the year before, the French warmed up for the tournament with a 2-0 defeat in two-Test home series against South Africa. What was worse was that this series culminated in a catastrophic 52-10 hammering at Parc des Princes by a touring side capable of playing top-class rugby at the highest speed. France were made to look second-rate as the Springboks ran in seven tries almost at will.

On the other hand, England, France's first Five Nations opponents, had taken comfort from their four pre-Christmas internationals, after drawing with Australia and, thrillingly, the all-powerful All Blacks. But the French are

> "The French are able to do many things after a big defeat. If we are proud, we can get a result."
> COACH PIERRE VILLEPREUX on the eve of the '98 campaign

Silver service – locks Olivier Brouzet, also top, and Fabien Pelous enjoy France's second Grand Slam in a row, secured thanks to the mastery of Castaignède, far right

KEY PLAYER 1998

Christian Califano

nothing if not unpredictable. The coaching duo of Jean-Claude Skrela and Pierre Villepreux made eight changes in the wake of the defeat against South Africa, plucking hooker Raphael Ibanez from obscurity to be captain on his full Five Nations debut in the tournament's first game at the new £270 million Stade de France in Paris.

The match finished 24-17 in France's favour, but in truth England should never have been that close, French finishing proving profligate, and almost, in the end, costing them the game.

France dominated in the forward exchanges, their front row routing England in the tight and loosehead prop Christian Califano particularly explosive in open play as well. Tries from right wing Philippe Bernat-Salles and then left wing Christophe Dominici on his debut helped France into a 15-3 half-time lead, but they should have had at least three more touchdowns as only missed chances and resolute defence kept England in the match.

The second half followed a similar pattern to the first as France continued to squander try-scoring chances, but this time England showed more of their mettle and, with a try from Neil Back, gradually fought their way back to 18-14 and 21-17. It took a drop goal by full back Jean-Luc Sadourny in the last minute to calm French fears.

France now travelled to Murrayfield with optimism that a second successive Grand Slam was possible, but also in the knowledge that the French national team had managed

> "We only scored two tries but that is deceptive. Our defence was solid – that was the key to it all. We were really motivated today and we did the simple things well."
>
> THOMAS CASTAIGNEDE
> on victory over England

Christian Califano can run 100 metres in 12 seconds and cover a 20-metre gap in a little over three. He has perfect passing technique, superb vision in open play and the knack for finding a gap. He is also a prop.

The Toulouse loosehead has the qualifications of a back, but the scrummaging power to see off any forward. And he is a driving force behind the resurgence of French rugby. He made his debut in New Zealand in 1994 against fearsome prop Richard Loe, but rather than be overawed by the occasion and the opponent, Califano outplayed him.

In the 1998 Grand Slam, he had a major role in helping France play the style of fast, open rugby that the South Africans had used to destroy them just months before. Rock solid in the scrum, Califano was also unstoppable in the loose, as three bulldozing runs against England in the opening game of the series demonstrated. Califano's club coach, Guy Noves, called him "the rugby player of the year 2000". He is sure to outpacing opponents well past that date.

Captain Raphael Ibanez is deservedly delighted after the exploits of stars such as Stephane Glas, right, and Christophe Lamaison, far right, had secured his team a place in Five Nations history

> "Everything you associate with French rugby – arrogance, panache, sublime skills and blistering pace – came together on the final afternoon of the tournament under a hot sun at Wembley. They destroyed Wales."
>
> BRENDAN GALLAGHER
> in 'Rugby Union 99'

Lièvremont managed to grab a brace of tries himself to cap a magnificent performance.

Given that the French had been such an irresistible force in Scotland, for Ireland to come to the Stade de France and battle to within seven minutes of an extraordinary victory seems bizarre, but they did and gave the whole of France a mighty shock.

The Irish were magnificent, stunning the home side with their workrate and passion. At one stage the French were staring at a 16-6 deficit, and with Ireland, unlike the Scots, giving their opponents little room to manoeuvre, a comeback looked improbable. But first a try from Bernat-Salles, his fourth of the championship, and then another score by Ibanez, crashing over from a lineout immediately after the Irish had squandered a good chance in the last ten minutes, brought France home to a third win of the season by a narrow 18-16.

So it was to Wembley, the temporary home of Wales, where the French turned to clinch their own twin towers of successive Grand Slams. And they produced a stunning performance to grace the old stadium, winning 51-0, their biggest ever victory and Wales's worst defeat.

Bleached-blond fly half Thomas Castaignede was the orchestrator of a Red rout, teasing and tormenting his opposite number Neil Jenkins as he ripped pitiful Wales

only one win on Scottish soil in the previous 20 years. Shrugging off an early 6-0 deficit, France quickly slipped into their free-flowing game and ran away with the match, outscoring Scotland by seven tries to one in a 51-16 win which was their highest ever Five Nations score and equalled their record margin of victory.

The mobile back row of the Lièvremont brothers and Olivier Magne was the foundation of the French dominance, and flanker Marc

> "It was one-sided but far from one-dimensional. Let us celebrate their performance because the French offered us treats and subtleties we barely knew existed. They threatened to score every time they handled the ball."
>
> DAVID WALSH, THE SUNDAY TIMES
> after Scotland were trounced at Murrayfield

Thomas Castaignède

Before the start of the Five Nations in 1998, French backs coach Pierre Villepreux had singled out fly half Thomas Castaignède as a vital piece in the French gameplan.

Remarkably, the Castres imp was still an amateur player for that tournament, an engineering degree taking up the majority of his time, but such was his performance throughout his second full Five Nations season that he ended up as the Heineken European Player of the Year.

Castaignède was the inspiration behind the sublime heights French rugby hit in 1998, orchestrating attacks with an all-round artistry that led some to hark back to the genius of Welsh fly halves such as Barry John and Phil Bennett.

Fast and skilful, Castaignède first came to prominence in French rugby in 1995 while still only 19, helping his country to a shock win over New Zealand. After his displays in the Five Nations he would appear to have the world at his feet.

apart and the Grand Slam was sealed in style with seven tries, Sadourny opening the floodgates after only three minutes. It was French rugby at its best, open, attacking play with Castaignède ably abetted by his scrum half Philippe Carbonneau. So comfortable was the victory that coach Skrela was able to replace both of them after 67 minutes to give his second string a go.

Critics and supporters hailed a team they thought could be France's greatest ever side. Sadly, it all went wrong in 1999…

Results and Statistics

Who did what, when, where and by how much: a comprehensive
list of Five Nations results plus all the record holders
in the Five Nations tournament for each competing country

Listed on these pages are the results between England, Scotland, Ireland, Wales and France since international rugby started. The Home Championship began in 1883, although in those days the teams rarely managed to all play each other. The Five Nations began in 1910, when France first played all the other teams, and the results listed here from 1910 onwards apply to the Five Nations Championship only.

Above: Thomas Castaignède converts a kick against Ireland in 1999

1871
Scotland 1G1T England 1T
(Raeburn Place, Edinburgh)
1872
England 1G 1DG 2T Scotland 1DG
(The Oval)
1873
England 0 Scotland 0 *(Glasgow)*
1874
England 1DG Scotland 1T *(The Oval)*
1875
Scotland 0 England 0
(Raeburn Place, Edinburgh)
England 1G 1DG 1T Ireland 0 *(The Oval)*
1876
England 1G 1T Scotland 0 *(The Oval)*
Ireland 0 England 1G1T *(Dublin)*
1877
Scotland 1T England 0
(Raeburn Place, Edinburgh)
England 2G 2T Ireland 0 *(The Oval)*
Ireland 0 Scotland 4G 2DG 2T *(Belfast)*
1878
England 0 Scotland 0 *(The Oval)*
Ireland 0 England 2G 1T *(Dublin)*
1879
Scotland 1DG England 1G
(Raeburn Place, Edinburgh)
England 2G 1DG 2T Ireland 0 *(The Oval)*
Ireland 0 Scotland 1G 1DG 1T *(Belfast)*
1880
England 2G 3T Scotland 1G *(Manchester)*
Ireland 1T England 2G2T *(Dublin)*
Scotland 1G 2DG 2T Ireland 0 *(Glasgow)*
1881
Scotland 1G 1T England 1DG 1T
(Raeburn Place, Edinburgh)
England 2G 2T Ireland 0 *(Manchester)*

England 7G 1DG 6T Wales 0 *(Blackheath)*
Ireland 1DG Scotland 1T *(Belfast)*
1882
England 0 Scotland 2T *(Manchester)*
Ireland 2T England 2t *(Dublin)*
Scotland 2T Ireland 0 *(Glasgow)*
Ireland 0 Wales 2G 2T *(Dublin)*
1883
Scotland 1T England 2T
(Raeburn Place, Edinburgh)
England 1G 3T Ireland 1T *(Manchester)*
Wales 0 England 2G 4T *(Swansea)*
Ireland 0 Scotland 1G 1T *(Belfast)*
Scotland 3G Wales 1G
(Raeburn Place, Edinburgh)
1884
Ireland 0 England 1G
(Lansdowne Road, Dublin)
England 1G Scotland 1T *(Manchester)*
England 1G 2T Wales 1G
(Cardigan Fields, Leeds)
Scotland 2G2T Ireland 1T
(Raeburn Place, Edinburgh)
Wales 2T 1DG Ireland 0 *(Cardiff Arms Park)*

Wales 0 Scotland 1T 1DG
(Rodney Parade, Newport)
1885
England 2T Ireland 1T *(Manchester)*
Wales 1G 1T England 1G 4T *(Swansea)*
Ireland 0 Scotland 1G 1T *(Belfast)*
Scotland 0 Wales 0
(Hamilton Crescent, Glasgow)
1886
Ireland 0 England 1T
(Lansdowne Road, Dublin)
Scotland 0 England 0
(Raeburn Place, Edinburgh)
England 2T 1GM Wales 1G
(Rectory Field, Blackheath)
Scotland 3G 2T 1DG Ireland 0
(Raeburn Place, Edinburgh)
Wales 0 Scotland 2G 1T
(Cardiff Arms Park)
1887
Ireland 2G England 0 *(Lansdowne Road)*
England 1T Scotland 1T
(Whalley Range, Manchester)
Wales 0 England 0 *(Stradey Park, Llanelli)*

HOW POINTS VALUES HAVE CHANGED IN A CENTURY OF INTERNATIONAL RUGBY						
	Try	Conversion	Penalty goal	Drop goal	Goal from mark	
1891	1	2	2	3	3	It wasn't until 1891
1892	2	3	3	4	4	that the countries
1894	3	2	3	4	4	agreed on how many
1905	3	2	3	4	3	points to award for a
1949	3	2	3	3	3	try and so on – hence
1972	4	2	3	3	3	scores like 7G 1DG 6T
1978	4	2	3	3	-	to nil (England's rout
1992	5	2	3	3	-	of Wales in 1881!)

Ireland 0 Scotland 1G 2T 1GM
(Ormeau, Belfast)
Wales 1T 1DG Ireland 3T *(Birkenhead Park)*
Scotland 4G 8T Wales 0
(Raeburn Place, Edinburgh)
1888
Scotland 1G Ireland 0
(Raeburn Place, Edinburgh)
Wales 1T Scotland 0
(Rodney Parade, Newport)
Ireland 1G 1T 1DG Wales 0
(Lansdowne Road)
1889
Ireland 1DG Scotland 0 *(Ormeau, Belfast)*
Wales 0 Ireland 2T *(St Helen's, Swansea)*
Scotland 2T Wales 0
(Raeburn Place, Edinburgh)
1890
England 3T Ireland 0
(Rectory Field, Blackheath)
Scotland 0 England 1G 1T
(Whalley Range, Manchester)
England 0 Wales 1T *(Crown Flatt, Dewsbury)*
Scotland 1T 1DG Ireland 0 *(Ormeau, Belfast)*
Ireland 1G Wales 1G *(Lansdowne Road, Dublin)*
Wales 1T Scotland 1G 2T *(Cardiff Arms Park)*
1891
Ireland 0 England 9 *(Lansdowne Road)*
England 3 Scotland 9 *(Athletic Ground, Richmond)*
Wales 3 England 7 *(Rodney Park, Newport)*
Ireland 0 Scotland 14 *(Ballynafeigh, Belfast)*
Wales 6 Ireland 4 *(Stradey Park, Llanelli)*
Scotland 15 Wales 0 *(Raeburn Place, Edinburgh)*
1892
England 7 Ireland 0 *(Whalley Ranger, Manchester)*
Scotland 0 England 5 *(Raeburn Place, Edinburgh)*
England 17 Wales 0 *(Rectory Field, Blackheath)*
Scotland 2 Ireland 0 *(Raeburn Place, Edinburgh)*
Ireland 9 Wales 0 *(Lansdowne Road)*
Wales 2 Scotland 7 *(St Helen's, Swansea)*
1893
Ireland 0 England 4 *(Lansdowne Road)*
England 0 Scotland 8 *(Headingley, Leeds)*
Wales 12 England 11 *(Cardiff Arms Park)*
Ireland 0 Scotland 0 *(Ballynafeigh, Belfast)*
Wales 2 Ireland 0 *(Stradey Park, Llanelli)*
Scotland 0 Wales 9 *(Raeburn Place, Edinburgh)*
1894
England 5 Ireland 7 *(Rectory Field, Blackheath)*
Scotland 6 England 0 *(Raeburn Place, Edinburgh)*

England 24 Wales 3 *(Birkenhead Park)*
Ireland 5 Scotland 0 *(Lansdowne Road)*
Ireland 3 Wales 0 *(Ballynafeigh, Belfast)*
Wales 7 Scotland 0 *(Rodney Parade, Newport)*
1895
Ireland 3 England 6 *(Lansdowne Road)*
England 3 Scotland 6 *(Athletic Ground, Richmond)*
Wales 6 England 14 *(St Helen's, Swansea)*
Scotland 6 Ireland 0 *(Raeburn Place, Edinburgh)*
Wales 5 Ireland 3 *(Cardiff Arms Park)*
Scotland 5 Wales 4 *(Raeburn Place, Edinburgh)*
1896
England 4 Ireland 10 *(Meanwood Road, Leeds)*
Scotland 11 England 0 *(Old Hampton Park, Glasgow)*
England 25 Wales 0 *(Rectory Field, Blackheath)*
Ireland 0 Scotland 0 *(Lansdowne Road)*
Ireland 8 Wales 4 *(Lansdowne Road)*
Wales 6 Scotland 0 *(Cardiff Arms Park)*
1897
Ireland 13 England 9 *(Lansdowne Road)*
England 12 Scotland 3 *(Fallowfield, Manchester)*
Wales 11 England 0 *(Rodney Parade, Newport)*
Scotland 8 Ireland 3 *(Powderhall, Edinburgh)*
1898
England 6 Ireland 9 *(Athletic Ground, Richmond)*
Scotland 3 England 3 *(Powderhall, Edinburgh)*
England 14 Wales 7 *(Rectory Field, Blackheath)*
Ireland 0 Scotland 8
(Balmoral Showgrounds, Belfast)
Ireland 3 Wales 11 *(Limerick)*
1899
Ireland 6 England 0 *(Lansdowne Road)*
England 0 Scotland 5 *(Rectory Field, Blackheath)*
Wales 29 England 3 *(St Helen's, Swansea)*
Scotland 3 Ireland 9 *(Inverleith, Edinburgh)*
Wales 0 Ireland 3 *(Cardiff Arms Park)*
Scotland 21 Wales 10 *(Inverleith, Edinburgh)*
1900
England 15 Ireland 4 *(Athletic Ground, Richmond)*
Scotland 0 England 0 *(Inverleith, Edinburgh)*
England 3 Wales 13 *(Kingsholm, Gloucester)*
Ireland 0 Scotland 0 *(Lansdowne Road)*
Ireland 0 Wales 3 *(Balmoral Showgrounds, Belfast)*
Wales 12 Scotland 3 *(St Helen's, Swansea)*
1901
Ireland 10 England 6 *(Lansdowne Road)*
England 3 Scotland 18 *(Rectory Field, Blackheath)*
Wales 13 England 0 *(Cardiff Arms Park)*
Scotland 9 Ireland 5 *(Inverleith, Edinburgh)*
Wales 10 Ireland 9 *(St Helen's, Swansea)*

Scotland 18 Wales 8 *(Inverleith, Edinburgh)*
1902
England 6 Ireland 3 *(Welford Road, Leicester)*
Scotland 3 England 6 *(Inverleith, Edinburgh)*
England 8 Wales 9 *(Rectory Field, Blackheath)*
Ireland 5 Scotland 0 *(Lansdowne Road)*
Ireland 0 Wales 15 *(Lansdowne Road)*
Wales 14 Scotland 5 *(Cardiff Arms Park)*
1903
Ireland 6 England 0 *(Lansdowne Road)*
England 6 Scotland 10 *(Athletic Ground, Richmond)*
Wales 21 England 5 *(St Helen's, Swansea)*
Scotland 3 Ireland 0 *(Inverleith, Edinburgh)*
Wales 18 Ireland 0 *(Cardiff Arms Park)*
Scotland 6 Wales 0 *(Inverleith, Edinburgh)*
1904
England 19 Ireland 0 *(Rectory Field, Blackheath)*
Scotland 6 England 3 *(Inverleith, Edinburgh)*
England 14 Wales 14 *(Welford Road, Leicester)*
Ireland 3 Scotland 19 *(Lansdowne Road)*
Ireland 14 Wales 12
(Balmoral Showgrounds, Belfast)
Wales 21 Scotland 3 *(St Helen's, Swansea)*
1905
Ireland 17 England 3 *(Mardyke, Cork)*
England 0 Scotland 8 *(Athletic Ground, Richmond)*
Wales 25 England 0 *(Cardiff Arms Park)*
Scotland 5 Ireland 11 *(Inverleith, Edinburgh)*
Wales 10 Ireland 3 *(Cardiff Arms Park)*
Scotland 3 Wales 6 *(Inverleith, Edinburgh)*
1906
England 19 Ireland 0 *(Rectory Field, Blackheath)*
Scotland 3 England 9 *(Inverleith, Edinburgh)*
England 3 Wales 16 *(Athletic Ground, Richmond)*
Ireland 6 Scotland 13 *(Lansdowne Road)*
Ireland 11 Wales 6 *(Balmoral Showgrounds, Belfast)*
Wales 9 Scotland 3 *(Cardiff Arms Park)*
France 8 England 35 *(Paris)*
1907
Ireland 17 England 9 *(Lansdowne Road)*
England 3 Scotland 8 *(Rectory Field, Blackheath)*
Wales 22 England 0 *(St Helen's, Swansea)*
Scotland 15 Ireland 3 *(Inverleith, Edinburgh)*
Wales 29 Ireland 0 *(Cardiff Arms Park)*
Scotland 6 Wales 3 *(Inverleith, Edinburgh)*
England 41 France 13 *(Athletic Ground, Richmond)*
1908
England 13 Ireland 3 *(Athletic Ground, Richmond)*
England 28 Scotland 18 *(Ashton Gate, Bristol)*
England 14 Wales 14 *(Twickenham)*

Ireland 16 Scotland 11 *(Lansdowne Road)*
Ireland 5 Wales 11 *(Balmoral Showgrounds, Belfast)*
Wales 6 Scotland 5 *(St Helen's, Swansea)*
France 0 England 19 *(Paris)*
Wales 36 France 4 *(Cardiff)*

1909
Ireland 5 England 11 *(Lansdowne Road)*
England 8 Scotland 18 *(Athletic Ground, Richmond)*
Wales 8 England 0 *(Cardiff Arms Park)*
Scotland 9 Ireland 3 *(Inverleith, Edinburgh)*
Wales 18 Ireland 5 *(St Helen's, Swansea)*
Scotland 3 Wales 5 *(Inverleith, Edinburgh)*
England 22 France 0 *(Leicester)*
Ireland 19 France 8 *(Lansdowne Road)*
France 5 Wales 47 *(Paris)*

1910
England 0 Ireland 0 *(Twickenham)*
Scotland 5 England 14 *(Inverleith, Edinburgh)*
England 11 Wales 6 *(Twickenham)*
Ireland 0 Scotland 14 *(Lansdowne Road)*
Ireland 3 Wales 19 *(Lansdowne Road)*
Wales 14 Scotland 0 *(Cardiff Arms Park)*
France 3 England 11 *(Parc des Princes, Paris)*
France 3 Ireland 8 *(Parc des Princes, Paris)*
Scotland 27 France 0 *(Inverleith, Edinburgh)*
Wales 49 France 14 *(St Helen's, Swansea)*

1911
Ireland 3 England 0 *(Lansdowne Road)*
England 13 Scotland 8 *(Twickenham)*
Wales 15 England 11 *(St Helen's, Swansea)*
Scotland 10 Ireland 16 *(Inverleith, Edinburgh)*
Wales 16 Ireland 0 *(Cardiff Arms Park)*
Scotland 10 Wales 32 *(Inverleith, Edinburgh)*
England 37 France 0 *(Twickenham)*
Ireland 25 France 5 *(Mardyke, Cork)*

France 16 Scotland 15 *(Stade Colombes, Paris)*
France 0 Wales 15 *(Parc des Princes, Paris)*

1912
England 15 Ireland 0 *(Twickenham)*
Scotland 8 England 3 *(Inverleith, Edinburgh)*
England 8 Wales 0 *(Twickenham)*
Ireland 10 Scotland 8 *(Lansdowne Road)*
Ireland 12 Wales 5 *(Balmoral Showgrounds, Belfast)*
Wales 21 Scotland 6 *(St Helen's, Swansea)*
France 8 England 18 *(Parc des Princes, Paris)*
France 6 Ireland 11 *(Parc des Princes, Paris)*
Scotland 31 France 3 *(Inverleith, Edinburgh)*
Wales 14 France 8 *(Rodney Parade, Newport)*

1913
Ireland 4 England 15 *(Lansdowne Road)*
England 3 Scotland 0 *(Twickenham)*
Wales 0 England 12 *(Cardiff Arms Park)*
Scotland 29 Ireland 14 *(Inverleith, Edinburgh)*
Wales 16 Ireland 13 *(St Helen's, Swansea)*
Scotland 0 Wales 8 *(Inverleith, Edinburgh)*
England 20 France 0 *(Twickenham)*
Ireland 24 France 0 *(Mardyke, Cork)*
France 3 Scotland 21 *(Parc des Princes, Paris)*
France 8 Wales 11 *(Parc des Princes, Paris)*

1914
England 17 Ireland 12 *(Twickenham)*
Scotland 15 England 16 *(Inverleith, Edinburgh)*
England 10 Wales 9 *(Twickenham)*
Ireland 9 Scotland 9 *(Lansdowne Road)*
Ireland 3 Wales 11 *(Balmoral Showgrounds, Belfast)*
Wales 24 Scotland 5 *(Cardiff Arms Park)*
France 13 England 39 *(Stade Colombes, Paris)*
France 6 Ireland 8 *(Parc des Princes, Paris)*
Wales 31 France 0 *(St Helen's, Swansea)*

First World War

1920
Ireland 11 England 14 *(Lansdowne Road)*
England 13 Scotland 4 *(Twickenham)*
Wales 19 England 5 *(St Helen's, Swansea)*
Scotland 19 Ireland 0 *(Inverleith, Edinburgh)*
Wales 28 Ireland 4 *(Cardiff Arms Park)*
Scotland 9 Wales 5 *(Inverleith, Edinburgh)*
England 8 France 3 *(Twickenham)*
Ireland 7 France 15 *(Lansdowne Road)*
France 0 Scotland 5 *(Parc des Princes, Paris)*
France 5 Wales 6 *(Stade Colombes, Paris)*

1921
England 15 Ireland 0 *(Twickenham)*
Scotland 0 England 18 *(Inverleith, Edinburgh)*
England 18 Wales 3 *(Twickenham)*
Ireland 9 Scotland 9 *(Lansdowne Road)*
Ireland 0 Wales 6 *(Balmoral Showgrounds, Belfast)*
Wales 8 Scotland 14 *(St Helen's, Swansea)*
France 6 England 10 *(Stade Colombes, Paris)*
France 20 Ireland 10 *(Stade Colombes, Paris)*
Scotland 0 France 3 *(Inverleith, Edinburgh)*
Wales 12 France 4 *(Rodney Parade, Newport)*

1922
Ireland 3 England 12 *(Lansdowne Road)*
England 11 Scotland 5 *(Twickenham)*
Wales 28 England 6 *(Cardiff Arms Park)*
Scotland 6 Ireland 3 *(Inverleith, Edinburgh)*
Wales 11 Ireland 5 *(St Helen's, Swansea)*
Scotland 9 Wales 9 *(Inverleith, Edinburgh)*
England 11 France 11 *(Twickenham)*
Ireland 8 France 3 *(Lansdowne Road)*
France 3 Scotland 3 *(Stade Colombes, Paris)*
France 3 Wales 11 *(Stade Colombes, Paris)*

1923
England 23 Ireland 5 *(Welford Road, Leicester)*
Scotland 6 England 8 *(Inverleith, Edinburgh)*
England 7 Wales 3 *(Twickenham)*
Ireland 3 Scotland 13 *(Lansdowne Road)*
Ireland 5 Wales 4 *(Lansdowne Road)*
Wales 8 Scotland 11 *(Cardiff Arms Park)*
France 3 England 12 *(Stade Colombes, Paris)*
France 14 Ireland 8 *(Stade Colombes, Paris)*
Scotland 16 France 3 *(Inverleith, Edinburgh)*
Wales 16 France 8 *(St Helen's, Swansea)*

1924
Ireland 3 England 14 *(Ravenhill, Belfast)*
England 19 Scotland 0 *(Twickenham)*
Wales 9 England 17 *(St Helen's, Swansea)*
Scotland 13 Ireland 8 *(Inverleith, Edinburgh)*
Wales 10 Ireland 13 *(Cardiff Arms Park)*

1922: England v Wales at Cardiff – a Welsh forward tries to pass the ball before being flattened in the mud

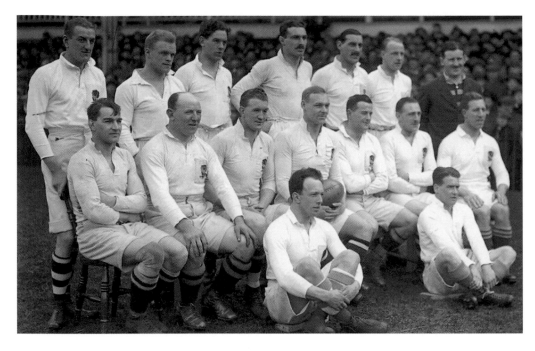

1924: The England team before playing Wales.
Left to right standing: H C Cakeside, B S Cantrell,
H P Jacob, R Cove-Smith, A F Blakison, H M Locke,
and referee A W Angers. Seated: G S Conway,
R Edwards, T Voyce, W W Wakefield, E Myers,
L J Corbett and W G E Luddington.
On the ground: A Robson and A F Young

Ireland 5 Wales 5 *(Ravenhill, Belfast)*
Wales 14 Scotland 7 *(St Helen's, Swansea)*
France 6 England 16 *(Stade Colombes, Paris)*
France 0 Ireland 6 *(Yves du Manor Stadium, Paris)*
Scotland 6 France 3 *(Murrayfield)*
Wales 8 France 3 *(Cardiff Arms Park)*
1930
Ireland 4 England 3 *(Lansdowne Road)*
England 0 Scotland 0 *(Twickenham)*
Wales 3 England 11 *(Cardiff Arms Park)*
Scotland 11 Ireland 14 *(Murrayfield)*
Wales 12 Ireland 7 *(St Helen's, Swansea)*
Scotland 12 Wales 9 *(Murrayfield)*
England 11 France 5 *(Twickenham)*
Ireland 0 France 5 *(Ravenhill, Belfast)*
France 7 Scotland 3 *(Stade Colombes, Paris)*
France 0 Wales 11 *(Stade Colombes, Paris)*
1931
England 5 Ireland 6 *(Twickenham)*
Scotland 28 England 19 *(Murrayfield)*
England 11 Wales 11 *(Twickenham)*
Ireland 8 Scotland 5 *(Lansdowne Road)*
Ireland 3 Wales 15 *(Ravenhill, Belfast)*
Wales 13 Scotland 8 *(Cardiff Arms Park)*
France 14 England 13 *(Stade Colombes, Paris)*
France 3 Ireland 0 *(Stade Colombes, Paris)*
Scotland 6 France 4 *(Murrayfield)*
Wales 35 France 3 *(St Helen's, Swansea)*
1932
Ireland 8 England 11 *(Lansdowne Road)*
England 16 Scotland 3 *(Twickenham)*
Wales 12 England 5 *(St Helen's, Swansea)*
Scotland 8 Ireland 20 *(Murrayfield)*
Wales 10 Ireland 12 *(Cardiff Arms Park)*
Scotland 0 Wales 6 *(Murrayfield)*
1933
England 17 Ireland 6 *(Twickenham)*
Scotland 3 England 0 *(Murrayfield)*
England 3 Wales 7 *(Twickenham)*
Ireland 6 Scotland 8 *(Lansdowne Road)*
Ireland 10 Wales 5 *(Ravenhill, Belfast)*
Wales 3 Scotland 11 *(St Helen's, Swansea)*

Scotland 35 Wales 10 *(Inverleith, Edinburgh)*
England 19 France 7 *(Twickenham)*
Ireland 6 France 0 *(Lansdowne Road)*
France 12 Scotland 10 *(Stade Colombes, Paris)*
France 6 Wales 10 *(Stade Colombes, Paris)*
1925
England 6 Ireland 6 *(Twickenham)*
Scotland 14 England 11 *(Murrayfield)*
England 12 Wales 6 *(Twickenham)*
Ireland 8 Scotland 14 *(Lansdowne Road)*
Ireland 19 Wales 3 *(Ravenhill, Belfast)*
Wales 14 Scotland 24 *(St Helen's, Swansea)*
France 11 England 13 *(Stade Colombes, Paris)*
France 3 Ireland 9 *(Stade Colombes, Paris)*
Scotland 25 France 4 *(Inverleith, Edinburgh)*
Wales 11 France 5 *(Cardiff Arms Park)*
1926
Ireland 19 England 15 *(Lansdowne Road)*
England 9 Scotland 17 *(Twickenham)*
Wales 3 England 3 *(Cardiff Arms Park)*
Scotland 0 Ireland 3 *(Murrayfield)*
Wales 11 Ireland 8 *(St Helen's, Swansea)*
Scotland 8 Wales 5 *(Murrayfield)*
England 11 France 0 *(Twickenham)*
Ireland 11 France 0 *(Ravenhill, Belfast)*
France 6 Scotland 12 *(Stade Colombes, Paris)*
France 5 Wales 7 *(Stade Colombes, Paris)*

1927
England 8 Ireland 6 *(Twickenham)*
Scotland 21 England 13 *(Murrayfield)*
England 11 Wales 9 *(Twickenham)*
Ireland 6 Scotland 0 *(Lansdowne Road)*
Ireland 19 Wales 9 *(Lansdowne Road)*
Wales 0 Scotland 5 *(Cardiff Arms Park)*
France 3 England 0 *(Stade Colombes, Paris)*
France 3 Ireland 8 *(Stade Colombes, Paris)*
Scotland 23 France 6 *(Murrayfield)*
Wales 25 France 7 *(St Helen's, Swansea)*
1928
Ireland 6 England 7 *(Lansdowne Road)*
England 6 Scotland 0 *(Twickenham)*
Wales 8 England 10 *(St Helen's, Swansea)*
Scotland 5 Ireland 13 *(Murrayfield)*
Wales 10 Ireland 13 *(Cardiff Arms Park)*
Scotland 0 Wales 13 *(Murrayfield)*
England 18 France 8 *(Twickenham)*
Ireland 12 France 8 *(Ravenhill, Belfast)*
France 6 Scotland 15 *(Stade Colombes, Paris)*
France 8 Wales 3 *(Stade Colombes, Paris)*
1929
England 5 Ireland 6 *(Twickenham)*
Scotland 12 England 6 *(Murrayfield)*
England 8 Wales 3 *(Twickenham)*
Ireland 7 Scotland 16 *(Lansdowne Road)*

1951: Ireland v England in Dublin. The players leap for the ball during a lineout. That year the title 'Team of the Year' undoubtedly went to Ireland. Apart from a superior record to their rivals, the Irish side had done more to revive open, fast play than any other international team

1934

Ireland 3 England 13 *(Lansdowne Road)*
England 6 Scotland 3 *(Twickenham)*
Wales 0 England 9 *(Cardiff Arms Park)*
Scotland 16 Ireland 9 *(Murrayfield)*
Wales 13 Ireland 0 *(St Helen's, Swansea)*
Scotland 6 Wales 13 *(Murrayfield)*

1935

England 14 Ireland 3 *(Twickenham)*
Scotland 10 England 7 *(Murrayfield)*
England 3 Wales 3 *(Twickenham)*
Ireland 12 Scotland 5 *(Lansdowne Road)*
Ireland 9 Wales 3 *(Ravenhill, Belfast)*
Wales 10 Scotland 6 *(Cardiff Arms Park)*

1936

Ireland 6 England 3 *(Lansdowne Road)*
England 9 Scotland 8 *(Twickenham)*
Wales 0 England 0 *(St Helen's, Swansea)*
Scotland 4 Ireland 10 *(Murrayfield)*
Wales 3 Ireland 0 *(Cardiff Arms Park)*
Scotland 3 Wales 13 *(Murrayfield)*

1937

England 0 Ireland 5 *(Twickenham)*
Scotland 3 England 6 *(Murrayfield)*
England 4 Wales 3 *(Twickenham)*
Ireland 11 Scotland 4 *(Lansdowne Road)*
Ireland 5 Wales 3 *(Ravenhill, Belfast)*
Wales 6 Scotland 13 *(St Helen's, Swansea)*

1938

Ireland 14 England 36 *(Lansdowne Road)*
England 16 Scotland 21 *(Twickenham)*
Wales 14 England 8 *(Cardiff Arms Park)*
Scotland 23 Ireland 14 *(Murrayfield)*
Wales 11 Ireland 5 *(St Helen's, Swansea)*

Scotland 8 Wales 6 *(Murrayfield)*

1939

England 0 Ireland 5 *(Twickenham)*
Scotland 6 England 9 *(Murrayfield)*
England 3 Wales 0 *(Twickenham)*
Ireland 12 Scotland 3 *(Lansdowne Road)*
Ireland 0 Wales 7 *(Ravenhill, Belfast)*
Wales 11 Scotland 3 *(Cardiff Arms Park)*

Second World War

1947

Ireland 22 England 0 *(Lansdowne Road)*
England 24 Scotland 5 *(Twickenham)*
Wales 6 England 9 *(Cardiff Arms Park)*
Scotland 0 Ireland 3 *(Murrayfield)*
Wales 6 Ireland 0 *(St Helen's, Swansea)*
Scotland 8 Wales 22 *(Murrayfield)*
England 6 France 3 *(Twickenham)*
Ireland 8 France 12 *(Lansdowne Road)*
France 8 Scotland 3 *(Stade Colombes, Paris)*
France 0 Wales 3 *(Stade Colombes, Paris)*

1948

England 10 Ireland 11 *(Twickenham)*
Scotland 6 England 3 *(Murrayfield)*
England 3 Wales 3 *(Twickenham)*
Ireland 6 Scotland 0 *(Lansdowne Road)*
Ireland 6 Wales 3 *(Ravenhill, Belfast)*
Wales 14 Scotland 0 *(Cardiff Arms Park)*
France 15 England 0 *(Stade Colombes, Paris)*
France 6 Ireland 13 *(Stade Colombes, Paris)*
Scotland 9 France 8 *(Murrayfield)*
Wales 3 France 11 *(St Helen's, Swansea)*

1949

Ireland 14 England 5 *(Lansdowne Road)*
England 19 Scotland 3 *(Twickenham)*

Wales 9 England 3 *(Cardiff Arms Park)*
Scotland 3 Ireland 13 *(Murrayfield)*
Wales 0 Ireland 5 *(St Helen's, Swansea)*
Scotland 6 Wales 5 *(Murrayfield)*
England 8 France 3 *(Twickenham)*
Ireland 9 France 16 *(Lansdowne Road)*
France 0 Scotland 8 *(Stade Colombes, Paris)*
France 5 Wales 3 *(Stade Colombes, Paris)*

1950

England 3 Ireland 0 *(Twickenham)*
Scotland 13 England 11 *(Murrayfield)*
England 5 Wales 11 *(Twickenham)*
Ireland 21 Scotland 0 *(Lansdowne Road)*
Ireland 3 Wales 6 *(Ravenhill, Belfast)*
Wales 12 Scotland 0 *(St Helen's, Swansea)*
France 6 England 3 *(Stade Colombes, Paris)*
France 3 Ireland 3 *(Stade Colombes, Paris)*
Scotland 8 France 5 *(Murrayfield)*
Wales 21 France 0 *(Cardiff Arms Park)*

1951

Ireland 3 England 0 *(Lansdowne Road)*
England 5 Scotland 3 *(Twickenham)*
Wales 23 England 5 *(St Helen's, Swansea)*
Scotland 5 Ireland 6 *(Murrayfield)*
Wales 3 Ireland 3 *(Cardiff Arms Park)*
Scotland 19 Wales 0 *(Murrayfield)*
England 3 France 11 *(Twickenham)*
Ireland 9 France 8 *(Lansdowne Road)*
France 14 Scotland 12 *(Stade Colombes, Paris)*
France 8 Wales 3 *(Stade Colombes, Paris)*

1952

England 3 Ireland 0 *(Twickenham)*
Scotland 3 England 19 *(Murrayfield)*
England 6 Wales 8 *(Twickenham)*

Ireland 12 Scotland 8 *(Lansdowne Road)*
Ireland 3 Wales 14 *(Lansdowne Road)*
Wales 11 Scotland 0 *(Cardiff Arms Park)*
France 3 England 6 *(Stade Colombes, Paris)*
France 8 Ireland 11 *(Stade Colombes, Paris)*
Scotland 11 France 13 *(Murrayfield)*
Wales 9 France 5 *(St Helen's, Swansea)*
1953
Ireland 9 England 9 *(Lansdowne Road)*
England 26 Scotland 8 *(Twickenham)*
Wales 3 England 8 *(Cardiff Arms Park)*
Scotland 8 Ireland 26 *(Murrayfield)*
Wales 5 Ireland 3 *(St Helen's, Swansea)*
Scotland 0 Wales 12 *(Murrayfield)*
England 11 France 0 *(Twickenham)*
Ireland 16 France 3 *(Lansdowne Road)*
France 11 Scotland 5 *(Stade Colombes, Paris)*
France 3 Wales 6 *(Stade Colombes, Paris)*
1954
England 14 Ireland 3 *(Twickenham)*
Scotland 3 England 13 *(Murrayfield)*
England 9 Wales 6 *(Twickenham)*
Ireland 6 Scotland 0 *(Lansdowne Road)*
Ireland 9 Wales 12 *(Lansdowne Road)*
Wales 15 Scotland 3 *(St Helen's, Swansea)*
France 11 England 3 *(Stade Colombes, Paris)*
France 8 Ireland 0 *(Stade Colombes, Paris)*
Scotland 0 France 3 *(Murrayfield)*
Wales 19 France 13 *(Cardiff Arms Park)*
1955
Ireland 6 England 6 *(Lansdowne Road)*
England 9 Scotland 6 *(Twickenham)*

Wales 3 England 0 *(Cardiff Arms Park)*
Scotland 12 Ireland 3 *(Murrayfield)*
Wales 21 Ireland 3 *(Cardiff Arms Park)*
Scotland 14 Wales 8 *(Murrayfield)*
England 9 France 16 *(Twickenham)*
Ireland 3 France 5 *(Lansdowne Road)*
France 15 Scotland 0 *(Stade Colombes, Paris)*
France 11 Wales 16 *(Stade Colombes, Paris)*
1956
England 20 Ireland 0 *(Twickenham)*
Scotland 6 England 11 *(Murrayfield)*
England 3 Wales 8 *(Twickenham)*
Ireland 14 Scotland 10 *(Lansdowne Road)*
Ireland 11 Wales 3 *(Lansdowne Road)*
Wales 9 Scotland 3 *(Cardiff Arms Park)*
France 14 England 9 *(Stade Colombes, Paris)*
France 14 Ireland 8 *(Stade Colombes, Paris)*
Scotland 12 France 0 *(Murrayfield)*
Wales 5 France 3 *(Cardiff Arms Park)*
1957
Ireland 0 England 6 *(Lansdowne Road)*
England 16 Scotland 3 *(Twickenham)*
Wales 0 England 3 *(Cardiff Arms Park)*
Scotland 3 Ireland 5 *(Murrayfield)*
Wales 6 Ireland 5 *(Cardiff Arms Park)*
Scotland 9 Wales 6 *(Murrayfield)*
England 9 France 5 *(Twickenham)*
Ireland 11 France 6 *(Lansdowne Road)*
France 0 Scotland 6 *(Stade Colombes, Paris)*
France 13 Wales 19 *(Stade Colombes, Paris)*
1958
England 6 Ireland 0 *(Twickenham)*

Scotland 3 England 3 *(Murrayfield)*
England 3 Wales 3 *(Twickenham)*
Ireland 12 Scotland 6 *(Lansdowne Road)*
Ireland 6 Wales 9 *(Lansdowne Road)*
Wales 8 Scotland 3 *(Cardiff Arms Park)*
France 0 England 14 *(Stade Colombes, Paris)*
France 11 Ireland 6 *(Stade Colombes, Paris)*
Scotland 11 France 9 *(Murrayfield)*
Wales 6 France 16 *(Cardiff Arms Park)*
1959
Ireland 0 England 3 *(Lansdowne Road)*
England 3 Scotland 3 *(Twickenham)*
Wales 5 England 0 *(Cardiff Arms Park)*
Scotland 12 Ireland 6 *(Murrayfield)*
Wales 8 Ireland 6 *(Cardiff Arms Park)*
Scotland 6 Wales 5 *(Murrayfield)*
England 3 France 3 *(Twickenham)*
Ireland 9 France 5 *(Lansdowne Road)*
France 9 Scotland 0 *(Stade Colombes, Paris)*
France 11 Wales 3 *(Stade Colombes, Paris)*
1960
England 8 Ireland 5 *(Twickenham)*
Scotland 12 England 21 *(Murrayfield)*
England 14 Wales 6 *(Twickenham)*
Ireland 5 Scotland 6 *(Lansdowne Road)*
Ireland 9 Wales 10 *(Lansdowne Road)*
Wales 8 Scotland 0 *(Cardiff Arms Park)*
France 3 England 3 *(Stade Colombes, Paris)*
France 23 Ireland 6 *(Stade Colombes, Paris)*
Scotland 11 France 13 *(Murrayfield)*
Wales 8 France 16 *(Cardiff Arms Park)*
1961
Ireland 11 England 8 *(Lansdowne Road)*
England 6 Scotland 0 *(Twickenham)*
Wales 6 England 3 *(Cardiff Arms Park)*
Scotland 16 Ireland 8 *(Murrayfield)*
Wales 9 Ireland 0 *(Cardiff Arms Park)*
Scotland 3 Wales 0 *(Murrayfield)*
England 5 France 5 *(Twickenham)*
Ireland 3 France 15 *(Lansdowne Road)*
France 11 Scotland 0 *(Stade Colombes, Paris)*
France 8 Wales 6 *(Stade Colombes, Paris)*
1962
England 16 Ireland 0 *(Twickenham)*
Scotland 3 England 3 *(Murrayfield)*
England 0 Wales 0 *(Twickenham)*
Ireland 6 Scotland 20 *(Lansdowne Road)*
Ireland 3 Wales 3 *(Lansdowne Road)*
Wales 3 Scotland 8 *(Cardiff Arms Park)*
France 13 England 0 *(Stade Colombes, Paris)*

1959: France on their way to beating Scotland 9-0 at the Stade Colombes, Paris

1972: France beat England 37-12 at the Stade Colombes in Paris

France 11 Ireland 0 *(Stade Colombes, Paris)*
Scotland 3 France 11 *(Murrayfield)*
Wales 3 France 0 *(Cardiff Arms Park)*
1963
Ireland 0 England 0 *(Lansdowne Road)*
England 10 Scotland 8 *(Twickenham)*
Wales 6 England 13 *(Cardiff Arms Park)*
Scotland 3 Ireland 0 *(Murrayfield)*
Wales 6 Ireland 14 *(Cardiff Arms Park)*
Scotland 0 Wales 6 *(Murrayfield)*
England 6 France 5 *(Twickenham)*
Ireland 5 France 24 *(Lansdowne Road)*
France 6 Scotland 11 *(Stade Colombes, Paris)*
France 5 Wales 3 *(Stade Colombes, Paris)*
1964
England 5 Ireland 18 *(Twickenham)*
Scotland 15 England 6 *(Murrayfield)*
England 6 Wales 6 *(Twickenham)*
Ireland 3 Scotland 6 *(Lansdowne Road)*
Ireland 6 Wales 15 *(Lansdowne Road)*
Wales 11 Scotland 3 *(Cardiff Arms Park)*
France 3 England 6 *(Stade Colombes, Paris)*
France 27 Ireland 6 *(Stade Colombes, Paris)*
Scotland 10 France 0 *(Murrayfield)*
Wales 11 France 11 *(Cardiff Arms Park)*
1965
Ireland 5 England 0 *(Lansdowne Road)*
England 3 Scotland 3 *(Twickenham)*
Wales 14 England 3 *(Cardiff Arms Park)*
Scotland 6 Ireland 16 *(Murrayfield)*
Wales 14 Ireland 8 *(Cardiff Arms Park)*
Scotland 12 Wales 14 *(Murrayfield)*
England 6 France 5 *(Twickenham)*

Ireland 3 France 3 *(Lansdowne Road)*
France 16 Scotland 8 *(Stade Colombes, Paris)*
France 22 Wales 13 *(Stade Colombes, Paris)*
1966
England 6 Ireland 6 *(Twickenham)*
Scotland 6 England 3 *(Murrayfield)*
England 6 Wales 11 *(Twickenham)*
Ireland 3 Scotland 11 *(Lansdowne Road)*
Ireland 9 Wales 6 *(Lansdowne Road)*
Wales 8 Scotland 3 *(Cardiff Arms Park)*
France 13 England 0 *(Stade Colombes, Paris)*
France 11 Ireland 6 *(Stade Colombes, Paris)*
Scotland 3 France 3 *(Murrayfield)*
Wales 9 France 8 *(Cardiff Arms Park)*
1967
Ireland 3 England 8 *(Lansdowne Road)*
England 27 Scotland 14 *(Twickenham)*
Wales 34 England 21 *(Cardiff Arms Park)*
Scotland 3 Ireland 5 *(Murrayfield)*
Wales 0 Ireland 3 *(Cardiff Arms Park)*
Scotland 11 Wales 5 *(Murrayfield)*
England 12 France 16 *(Twickenham)*
Ireland 6 France 11 *(Lansdowne Road)*
France 8 Scotland 9 *(Stade Colombes, Paris)*
France 20 Wales 14 *(Stade Colombes, Paris)*
1968
England 9 Ireland 9 *(Twickenham)*
Scotland 6 England 8 *(Murrayfield)*
England 11 Wales 11 *(Twickenham)*
Ireland 14 Scotland 6 *(Lansdowne Road)*
Ireland 9 Wales 6 *(Lansdowne Road)*
Wales 5 Scotland 0 *(Cardiff Arms Park)*
France 14 England 9 *(Stade Colombes, Paris)*

France 16 Ireland 6 *(Stade Colombes, Paris)*
Scotland 6 France 8 *(Murrayfield)*
Wales 9 France 14 *(Cardiff Arms Park)*
1969
Ireland 17 England 5 *(Lansdowne Road)*
England 8 Scotland 3 *(Twickenham)*
Wales 30 England 9 *(Cardiff Arms Park)*
Scotland 0 Ireland 16 *(Murrayfield)*
Wales 3 Ireland 17 *(Cardiff Arms Park)*
Scotland 6 Wales 5 *(Murrayfield)*
England 22 France 8 *(Twickenham)*
Ireland 17 France 9 *(Lansdowne Road)*
France 3 Scotland 6 *(Stade Colombes, Paris)*
France 8 Wales 8 *(Stade Colombes, Paris)*
1970
England 9 Ireland 3 *(Twickenham)*
Scotland 14 England 5 *(Murrayfield)*
England 13 Wales 17 *(Twickenham)*
Ireland 16 Scotland 11 *(Lansdowne Road)*
Ireland 14 Wales 0 *(Lansdowne Road)*
Wales 18 Scotland 9 *(Cardiff Arms Park)*
France 35 England 13 *(Stade Colombes, Paris)*
France 8 Ireland 0 *(Stade Colombes, Paris)*
Scotland 9 France 11 *(Murrayfield)*
Wales 11 France 6 *(Cardiff Arms Park)*
1971
Ireland 6 England 9 *(Lansdowne Road)*
England 15 Scotland 16 *(Twickenham)*
Wales 22 England 6 *(Cardiff Arms Park)*
Scotland 5 Ireland 17 *(Murrayfield)*
Wales 23 Ireland 9 *(Cardiff Arms Park)*
Scotland 18 Wales 19 *(Murrayfield)*
England 14 France 14 *(Twickenham)*
Ireland 9 France 9 *(Lansdowne Road)*
France 13 Scotland 8 *(Stade Colombes, Paris)*
France 5 Wales 9 *(Stade Colombes, Paris)*
1972 (Troubles in Ireland meant the programme was incomplete)
England 12 Ireland 16 *(Twickenham)*
Scotland 23 England 9 *(Murrayfield)*
England 3 Wales 12 *(Twickenham)*
Wales 35 Scotland 12 *(Cardiff Arms Park)*
France 37 England 12 *(Stade Colombes, Paris)*
France 9 Ireland 14 *(Stade Colombes, Paris)*
Scotland 20 France 9 *(Murrayfield)*
Wales 20 France 6 *(Cardiff Arms Park)*
1973
Ireland 18 England 9 *(Lansdowne Road)*
England 20 Scotland 13 *(Twickenham)*
Wales 25 England 9 *(Cardiff Arms Park)*

Scotland 19 Ireland 14 *(Murrayfield)*
Wales 16 Ireland 12 *(Cardiff Arms Park)*
Scotland 10 Wales 9 *(Murrayfield)*
England 14 France 6 *(Twickenham)*
Ireland 6 France 4 *(Lansdowne Road)*
France 16 Scotland 13 *(Parc des Princes, Paris)*
France 12 Wales 3 *(Parc des Princes, Paris)*

1974

England 21 Ireland 26 *(Twickenham)*
Scotland 16 England 14 *(Murrayfield)*
England 16 Wales 12 *(Twickenham)*
Ireland 9 Scotland 6 *(Lansdowne Road)*
Ireland 9 Wales 9 *(Lansdowne Road)*
Wales 6 Scotland 0 *(Cardiff Arms Park)*
France 12 England 12 *(Parc des Princes, Paris)*
France 9 Ireland 6 *(Parc des Princes, Paris)*
Scotland 19 France 6 *(Murrayfield)*
Wales 16 France 16 *(Cardiff Arms Park)*

1975

Ireland 12 England 9 *(Lansdowne Road)*
England 7 Scotland 6 *(Twickenham)*
Wales 20 England 4 *(Cardiff Arms Park)*
Scotland 20 Ireland 13 *(Murrayfield)*
Wales 32 Ireland 4 *(Cardiff Arms Park)*
Scotland 12 Wales 10 *(Murrayfield)*
England 20 France 27 *(Twickenham)*
Ireland 25 France 6 *(Lansdowne Road)*
France 10 Scotland 9 *(Parc des Princes, Paris)*
France 10 Wales 25 *(Parc des Princes, Paris)*

1976

England 12 Ireland 13 *(Twickenham)*
Scotland 22 England 12 *(Murrayfield)*

England 9 Wales 21 *(Twickenham)*
Ireland 6 Scotland 15 *(Lansdowne Road)*
Ireland 9 Wales 34 *(Lansdowne Road)*
Wales 28 Scotland 6 *(Cardiff Arms Park)*
France 30 England 9 *(Parc des Princes, Paris)*
France 26 Ireland 3 *(Parc des Princes, Paris)*
Scotland 6 France 13 *(Murrayfield)*
Wales 19 France 13 *(Cardiff Arms Park)*

1977

Ireland 0 England 4 *(Lansdowne Road)*
England 26 Scotland 6 *(Twickenham)*
Wales 14 England 9 *(Cardiff Arms Park)*
Scotland 21 Ireland 18 *(Murrayfield)*
Wales 25 Ireland 9 *(Cardiff Arms Park)*
Scotland 6 Wales 5 *(Murrayfield)*
England 3 France 4 *(Twickenham)*
Ireland 6 France 15 *(Lansdowne Road)*
France 23 Scotland 3 *(Parc des Princes, Paris)*
France 16 Wales 9 *(Parc des Princes, Paris)*

1978

England 15 Ireland 9 *(Twickenham)*
Scotland 0 England 15 *(Murrayfield)*
England 6 Wales 9 *(Twickenham)*
Ireland 12 Scotland 9 *(Lansdowne Road)*
Ireland 16 Wales 20 *(Lansdowne Road)*
Wales 22 Scotland 14 *(Cardiff Arms Park)*
France 15 England 6 *(Parc des Princes, Paris)*
France 10 Ireland 9 *(Parc des Princes, Paris)*
Scotland 16 France 19 *(Murrayfield)*
Wales 16 France 7 *(Cardiff Arms Park)*

1979

Ireland 12 England 7 *(Lansdowne Road)*

England 7 Scotland 7 *(Twickenham)*
Wales 27 England 3 *(Cardiff Arms Park)*
Scotland 11 Ireland 11 *(Murrayfield)*
Wales 24 Ireland 21 *(Cardiff Arms Park)*
Scotland 13 Wales 19 *(Murrayfield)*
England 7 France 6 *(Twickenham)*
Ireland 9 France 9 *(Lansdowne Road)*
France 21 Scotland 17 *(Parc des Princes, Paris)*
France 14 Wales 13 *(Parc des Princes, Paris)*

1980

England 24 Ireland 9 *(Twickenham)*
Scotland 18 England 30 *(Murrayfield)*
England 9 Wales 8 *(Twickenham)*
Ireland 22 Scotland 15 *(Lansdowne Road)*
Ireland 21 Wales 7 *(Lansdowne Road)*
Wales 17 Scotland 6 *(Cardiff Arms Park)*
France 13 England 17 *(Parc des Princes, Paris)*
France 19 Ireland 18 *(Parc des Princes, Paris)*
Scotland 22 France 14 *(Murrayfield)*
Wales 18 France 9 *(Cardiff Arms Park)*

1981

Ireland 6 England 10 *(Lansdowne Road)*
England 23 Scotland 17 *(Twickenham)*
Wales 21 England 19 *(Cardiff Arms Park)*
Scotland 10 Ireland 9 *(Murrayfield)*
Wales 9 Ireland 8 *(Cardiff Arms Park)*
Scotland 15 Wales 6 *(Murrayfield)*
England 12 France 16 *(Twickenham)*
Ireland 13 France 19 *(Lansdowne Road)*
France 16 Scotland 9 *(Parc des Princes, Paris)*
France 19 Wales 15 *(Parc des Princes, Paris)*

1982

England 15 Ireland 16 *(Twickenham)*
Scotland 9 England 9 *(Murrayfield)*
England 17 Wales 7 *(Twickenham)*
Ireland 21 Scotland 12 *(Lansdowne Road)*
Ireland 20 Wales 12 *(Lansdowne Road)*
Wales 18 Scotland 34 *(Cardiff Arms Park)*
France 15 England 27 *(Parc des Princes, Paris)*
France 22 Ireland 9 *(Parc des Princes, Paris)*
Scotland 16 France 7 *(Murrayfield)*
Wales 22 France 12 *(Cardiff Arms Park)*

1983

Ireland 25 England 15 *(Lansdowne Road)*
England 12 Scotland 22 *(Twickenham)*
Wales 13 England 13 *(Cardiff Arms Park)*
Scotland 13 Ireland 15 *(Murrayfield)*
Wales 23 Ireland 9 *(Cardiff Arms Park)*
Scotland 15 Wales 19 *(Murrayfield)*
England 15 France 19 *(Twickenham)*

1981: France beat Wales 19-15 at the Parc des Princes, Paris, as part of the Grand Slam

Ireland 22 France 16 *(Lansdowne Road)*
France 19 Scotland 15 *(Parc des Princes, Paris)*
France 16 Wales 9 *(Parc des Princes, Paris)*
1984
England 12 Ireland 9 *(Twickenham)*
Scotland 18 England 6 *(Murrayfield)*
England 15 Wales 24 *(Twickenham)*

The different national venues provide very different
and distinctive atmospheres on match day. From top:
Lansdowne Road, Twickenham and Murrayfield

Ireland 9 Scotland 32 *(Lansdowne Road)*
Ireland 9 Wales 18 *(Lansdowne Road)*
Wales 9 Scotland 15 *(Cardiff Arms Park)*
France 32 England 18 *(Parc des Princes, Paris)*
France 25 Ireland 12 *(Parc des Princes, Paris)*
Scotland 21 France 12 *(Murrayfield)*
Wales 16 France 21 *(Cardiff Arms Park)*
1985
Ireland 13 England 10 *(Lansdowne Road)*
England 10 Scotland 7 *(Twickenham)*
Wales 24 England 15 *(Cardiff Arms Park)*
Scotland 15 Ireland 18 *(Murrayfield)*
Wales 9 Ireland 21 *(Cardiff Arms Park)*
Scotland 21 Wales 25 *(Murrayfield)*
England 9 France 9 *(Twickenham)*
Ireland 15 France 15 *(Lansdowne Road)*
France 11 Scotland 3 *(Parc des Princes, Paris)*
France 14 Wales 3 *(Parc des Princes, Paris)*
1986
England 25 Ireland 20 *(Twickenham)*
Scotland 33 England 6 *(Murrayfield)*
England 21 Wales 18 *(Twickenham)*
Ireland 9 Scotland 10 *(Lansdowne Road)*
Ireland 12 Wales 19 *(Lansdowne Road)*
Wales 22 Scotland 15 *(Cardiff Arms Park)*
France 29 England 10 *(Parc des Princes, Paris)*
France 29 Ireland 9 *(Parc des Princes, Paris)*
Scotland 18 France 17 *(Murrayfield)*
Wales 15 France 23 *(Cardiff Arms Park)*
1987
Ireland 17 England 0 *(Lansdowne Road)*
England 21 Scotland 12 *(Twickenham)*
Wales 19 England 12 *(Cardiff Arms Park)*
Scotland 16 Ireland 12 *(Murrayfield)*
Wales 11 Ireland 15 *(Cardiff Arms Park)*
Scotland 21 Wales 14 *(Murrayfield)*
England 15 France 19 *(Twickenham)*
Ireland 13 France 19 *(Lansdowne Road)*
France 28 Scotland 22 *(Parc des Princes, Paris)*
France 16 Wales 9 *(Parc des Princes, Paris)*
1988
England 35 Ireland 3 *(Twickenham)*
Scotland 6 England 9 *(Murrayfield)*
England 3 Wales 11 *(Twickenham)*
Ireland 22 Scotland 18 *(Lansdowne Road)*
Ireland 9 Wales 12 *(Lansdowne Road)*
Wales 25 Scotland 20 *(Cardiff Arms Park)*
France 10 England 9 *(Parc des Princes, Paris)*
France 25 Ireland 6 *(Parc des Princes, Paris)*
Scotland 23 France 12 *(Murrayfield)*

Wales 9 France 10 *(Cardiff Arms Park)*
1989
Ireland 3 England 16 *(Lansdowne Road)*
England 12 Scotland 12 *(Twickenham)*
Wales 12 England 9 *(Cardiff Arms Park)*
Scotland 37 Ireland 21 *(Murrayfield)*
Wales 13 Ireland 19 *(Cardiff Arms Park)*
Scotland 23 Wales 7 *(Murrayfield)*
England 11 France 0 *(Twickenham)*
Ireland 21 France 26 *(Lansdowne Road)*
France 19 Scotland 3 *(Parc des Princes, Paris)*
France 31 Wales 12 *(Parc des Princes, Paris)*
1990
England 23 Ireland 0 *(Twickenham)*
Scotland 13 England 7 *(Murrayfield)*
England 34 Wales 6 *(Twickenham)*
Ireland 10 Scotland 13 *(Lansdowne Road)*
Ireland 14 Wales 8 *(Lansdowne Road)*
Wales 9 Scotland 13 *(Cardiff Arms Park)*
France 7 England 26 *(Parc des Princes, Paris)*
France 31 Ireland 12 *(Parc des Princes, Paris)*
Scotland 22 France 14 *(Murrayfield)*
Wales 19 France 29 *(Cardiff Arms Park)*
1991
Ireland 7 England 16 *(Lansdowne Road)*
England 21 Scotland 12 *(Twickenham)*
Wales 6 England 25 *(Cardiff Arms Park)*
Scotland 28 Ireland 25 *(Murrayfield)*
Wales 21 Ireland 21 *(Cardiff Arms Park)*
Scotland 32 Wales 12 *(Murrayfield)*
England 21 France 19 *(Twickenham)*
Ireland 9 France 9 *(Lansdowne Road)*
France 15 Scotland 9 *(Parc des Princes, Paris)*
France 36 Wales 3 *(Parc des Princes, Paris)*
1992
England 38 Ireland 9 *(Twickenham)*
Scotland 7 England 25 *(Murrayfield)*
England 24 Wales 0 *(Twickenham)*
Ireland 10 Scotland 18 *(Lansdowne Road)*
Ireland 15 Wales 16 *(Lansdowne Road)*
Wales 15 Scotland 12 *(Cardiff Arms Park)*
France 13 England 31 *(Parc des Princes, Paris)*
France 19 Ireland 18 *(Parc des Princes, Paris)*
Scotland 10 France 6 *(Murrayfield)*
Wales 9 France 12 *(Cardiff Arms Park)*
1993
Ireland 17 England 3 *(Lansdowne Road)*
England 26 Scotland 12 *(Twickenham)*
Wales 10 England 9 *(Cardiff Arms Park)*
Scotland 15 Ireland 3 *(Murrayfield)*

Wales 14 Ireland 19 *(Cardiff Arms Park)*
Scotland 20 Wales 0 *(Murrayfield)*
England 16 France 15 *(Twickenham)*
Ireland 6 France 21 *(Lansdowne Road)*
France 11 Scotland 3 *(Parc des Princes, Paris)*
France 26 Wales 10 *(Parc des Princes, Paris)*

1994
England 12 Ireland 13 *(Twickenham)*
Scotland 14 England 15 *(Murrayfield)*
England 15 Wales 8 *(Twickenham)*
Ireland 6 Scotland 6 *(Lansdowne Road)*
Ireland 15 Wales 17 *(Lansdowne Road)*
Wales 29 Scotland 6 *(Cardiff Arms Park)*
France 14 England 18 *(Parc des Princes, Paris)*
France 35 Ireland 15 *(Parc des Princes, Paris)*
Scotland 12 France 20 *(Murrayfield)*
Wales 24 France 15 *(Cardiff Arms Park)*

1995
Ireland 8 England 20 *(Lansdowne Road)*
England 24 Scotland 12 *(Twickenham)*
Wales 9 England 23 *(Cardiff Arms Park)*
Scotland 26 Ireland 13 *(Murrayfield)*
Wales 12 Ireland 16 *(Cardiff Arms Park)*
Scotland 26 Wales 13 *(Murrayfield)*
England 31 France 10 *(Twickenham)*
Ireland 7 France 25 *(Lansdowne Road)*
France 21 Scotland 23 *(Parc des Princes, Paris)*
France 21 Wales 9 *(Parc des Princes, Paris)*

1996
England 28 Ireland 15 *(Twickenham)*
Scotland 9 England 18 *(Murrayfield)*
England 21 Wales 15 *(Twickenham)*
Ireland 10 Scotland 16 *(Lansdowne Road)*
Ireland 30 Wales 17 *(Lansdowne Road)*
Wales 14 Scotland 16 *(Cardiff Arms Park)*
France 15 England 12 *(Parc des Princes, Paris)*
France 45 Ireland 10 *(Parc des Princes, Paris)*
Scotland 19 France 14 *(Murrayfield)*
Wales 16 France 15 *(Cardiff Arms Park)*

1997
Ireland 6 England 46 *(Lansdowne Road)*
England 41 Scotland 13 *(Twickenham)*
Wales 13 England 34 *(Cardiff Arms Park)*
Scotland 38 Ireland 10 *(Murrayfield)*
Wales 25 Ireland 26 *(Cardiff Arms Park)*
Scotland 19 Wales 34 *(Murrayfield)*
England 20 France 23 *(Twickenham)*
Ireland 15 France 32 *(Lansdowne Road)*
France 47 Scotland 20 *(Parc des Princes, Paris)*
France 27 Wales 22 *(Parc des Princes, Paris)*

1998
England 35 Ireland 17 *(Twickenham)*
Scotland 20 England 34 *(Murrayfield)*
England 60 Wales 26 *(Twickenham)*
Ireland 16 Scotland 17 *(Lansdowne Road)*
Ireland 21 Wales 30 *(Lansdowne Road)*
Wales 19 Scotland 13 *(Wembley Stadium)*
France 24 England 17 *(Stade de France, Paris)*
France 18 Ireland 16 *(Stade de France, Paris)*
Scotland 16 France 51 *(Murrayfield)*
Wales 0 France 51 *(Wembley Stadium)*

1999
Ireland 15 England 27 *(Lansdowne Road)*
England 24 Scotland 21 *(Twickenham)*
Wales 32 England 31 *(Wembley Stadium)*
Scotland 30 Ireland 13 *(Murrayfield)*
Wales 23 Ireland 29 *(Wembley Stadium)*
Scotland 33 Wales 20 *(Murrayfield)*
England 21 France 10 *(Twickenham)*
Ireland 9 France 10 *(Lansdowne Road)*
France 22 Scotland 36 *(Stade de France, Paris)*
France 33 Wales 34 *(Stade de France, Paris)*

INTERNATIONAL CHAMPIONSHIP WINNERS

1883 England	1923 England	1964 Scotland and Wales
1884 England	1924 England	1965 Wales
1885 Matches not completed	1925 Scotland	1966 Wales
1886 England and Scotland	1926 Scotland and Ireland	1967 France
1887 Scotland	1927 Scotland and Ireland	1968 France
1888 Matches not completed	1928 England	1969 Wales
1889 Matches not completed	1929 Scotland	1970 Wales and France
1890 England and Scotland	1930 England	1971 Wales
1891 Scotland	1931 Wales	1972 Matches not completed
1892 England	1932 England, Wales, Ireland	1973 Quintuple tie
1893 Wales	1933 Scotland	1974 Ireland
1894 Ireland	1934 England	1975 Wales
1895 Scotland	1935 Ireland	1976 Wales
1896 Ireland	1936 Wales	1977 France
1897 Matches not completed	1937 England	1978 Wales
1898 Matches not completed	1938 Scotland	1979 Wales
1899 Ireland	1939 England, Wales and Ireland	1980 England
1900 Wales		1981 France
1901 Scotland	1947 Wales and England	1982 Ireland
1902 Wales	1948 Ireland	1983 France and Ireland
1903 Scotland	1949 Ireland	1984 Scotland
1904 Scotland	1950 Wales	1985 Ireland
1905 Wales	1951 Ireland	1986 France and Scotland
1906 Wales and Ireland	1952 Wales	1987 France
1907 Scotland	1953 England	1988 Wales and France
1908 Wales	1954 England, France and Wales	1989 France
1909 Wales		1990 Scotland
1910 England	1955 France and Wales	1991 England
1911 Wales	1956 Wales	1992 England
1912 England and Ireland	1957 England	1993 France
1913 England	1958 England	1994 Wales
1914 England	1959 France	1995 England
1920 England, Scotland and Wales	1960 France and England	1996 England
	1961 France	1997 France
1921 England	1962 France	1998 France
1922 Wales	1963 England	1999 Scotland

1925: The Scotland team before the game against Wales. This successful side won the Triple Crown and the Grand Slam

GRAND SLAM WINNERS
England – 11: 1913, 1914, 1921, 1923, 1924, 1928, 1934, 1937, 1954, 1957, 1960, 1980, 1991, 1992, 1995, 1996.
Wales – 8: 1908, 1909, 1911, 1950, 1952, 1971, 1976, 1978
France – 6: 1968, 1977, 1981, 1987, 1997, 1998
Scotland – 3: 1925, 1984, 1990
Ireland – 1: 1948

TRIPLE CROWN WINNERS
England – 21: 1883, 1884, 1892, 1913, 1914, 1921, 1923, 1924, 1928, 1934, 1937, 1954, 1957, 1960, 1980, 1991, 1992, 1995, 1996, 1997, 1998.
Wales – 17: 1893, 1900, 1902, 1905, 1908, 1909, 1911, 1950, 1952, 1965, 1969, 1971, 1976, 1977, 1978, 1979, 1988.
Scotland – 10: 1891, 1895, 1901, 1903, 1907, 1925, 1933, 1938, 1984, 1990.
Ireland – 6: 1894, 1899, 1948, 1949, 1982, 1985.

COUNTRY v COUNTRY STATISTICS
England v Ireland
England won 58 lost 38 drawn 7
Biggest win (England): Ireland 6 England 46 Lansdowne Road, Dublin 1997
Biggest win (Ireland): Ireland 22 England 0 Lansdowne Road, Dublin 1947
England top try scorer against Ireland:
Rory Underwood 7 tries in 14 games
England top points scorer against Ireland:
Paul Grayson 57pts in 4 games
Ireland top try scorer vs England:
Michael Flynn 3 tries in 5 games
Ireland top points scorer vs England:
Ollie Campbell 41pts in 4 games

England v France
England won 36 lost 27 drawn 7
Biggest win (England): England 37 France 0 Twickenham 1911
Biggest win (France): France 37 England 12 Stade des Colombes 1972
England top try scorer against France:
Daniel Lambert 8 tries in 3 games
England top points scorer against France:
Rob Andrew 61 pts in 12 games
France top try scorer vs England:
Michel Crauste 4 tries in 9 games
France top points scorer vs England:
Thierry Lacroix 41 pts in 6 games

England v Wales
England won 43 lost 48 drawn 12
Biggest win (England): England 60 Wales 26 Twickenham 1998
Biggest win (Wales): Wales 0 England 25 Cardiff Arms Park 1905
England top try scorer against Wales:
Rory Underwood 6 tries in 14 games
England top points scorer against Wales:
Dusty Hare 58 pts in 6 games
Wales top try scorer vs England:
Dewi Bebb 6 tries in 8 games
Wales top points scorer against England:
Neil Jenkins 48 points in 8 games

England v Scotland
England won 55 lost 35 drawn 12
Biggest win (England): England 41 Scotland 13 (Twickenham) 1997
Biggest win (Scotland): Scotland 33 England 6 (Murrayfield) 1986
England top try scorer vs Scotland:
Kit Lowe 6 tries in 6 games
England top points scorer vs Scotland:
Paul Grayson 58pts in 3 games
Scotland top try scorer vs England:
Ian Smith 9 tries in 8 games
Scotland top points scorer vs England:
Gavin Hastings 65pts in 10 games

Scotland v Ireland
Scotland won 56 lost 44 drawn 5
Biggest win (Scotland): Scotland 38 Ireland 10 Murrayfield 1997
Biggest win (Ireland): Ireland 21 Scotland 0 Lansdowne Road 1950
Scotland top try scorer vs Ireland:
Roy Laidlaw 6 tries in 9 games
Scotland top pts scorer vs Ireland:
Gavin Hastings 75 pts in 10 games
Ireland top try scorer vs Scotland:
Alan Duggan 5 tries in 5 games
Ireland top pts scorer vs Scotland:
Michael Kiernan 56 pts in 9 games

Scotland v France
Scotland won 33 lost 34 drawn 2
Biggest win (Scotland): Scotland 31 France 3 Inverleith, Edinburgh 1912

Biggest win (France): Scotland 16 France 51
Murrayfield 1998
Scotland top try scorer vs France:
Ian Smith 6 tries in 6 games
Scotland top pts scorer vs France:
Gavin Hastings 116pts in 11 games
France top try scorer vs Scotland:
Serge Blanco 5 tries in 12 games
France top pts scorer vs Scotland:
Serge Blanco 42 pts in 12 games

Scotland v Wales

Scotland won 45 lost 56 drawn 2
Biggest win (Scotland): Scotland 35 Wales 10
Inverleith, Edinburgh 1924
Biggest win (Wales): Wales 35 Scotland 12
Cardiff Arms Park 1972
Scotland top try scorer vs Wales:
Ian Smith 8 tries in 8 games
Scotland top pts scorer vs Wales:
Gavin Hastings 77 pts in 9 games
Wales top try scorer vs Scotland:
Willie Llewellyn 7 tries in 6 games
Wales top pts scorer vs Scotland:
Neil Jenkins 65 pts in 8 games

Wales v Ireland

Wales won 57 lost 37 drawn 6
Biggest win (Wales): Wales 29 Ireland 0
(Cardiff Arms Park) 1925
Biggest win (Ireland): Ireland 19 Wales 3
(Ravenhill, Belfast) 1907
Top try scorer Wales vs Ireland:
John Williams 8 tries in 5 games
Top points scorer Wales vs Ireland:
Neil Jenkins 107 pts in 9 games
Top try scorer Ireland vs Wales:
James Ganly 3 tries in 2 games
Top points scorer Ireland vs Wales:
Eric Elwood 57 points in 6 games

Wales v France

Wales won 37 lost 30 drawn 3
Biggest win (Wales): Wales 49 France 14
St Helens, Swansea 1910
Biggest win (France): Wales 0 France 51
Wembley Stadium 1998
Wales top try scorer vs France:
Reggie Gibbs 7 tries in 3 games

1998: France v Wales at Wembley, London. Philippe Bernat-Salles on the run during France's biggest ever Five Nations victory over Wales (51-0)

Wales top pts scorer vs France:
Neil Jenkins 92pts in 10 games
France top try scorer vs Wales:
Serge Blanco 6 tries in 11 games
France top pts scorer vs Wales:
Jean-Baptiste Lafond 43pts in 8 games

Ireland v France

Ireland won 23 lost 42 drawn 5
Biggest win (Ireland): Ireland 24 France 0
Cork 1913
Biggest win (France): France 45 Ireland 10
Parc des Princes, Paris 1996
Ireland top try scorer vs France:
George Stephenson 11 tries in 11 games
Ireland top pts scorer vs France:
Michael Kiernan 73 pts in 9 games
France top try scorer vs Ireland:
Christian Darrouy 8 tries in 6 games
France top points scorer vs Ireland:
Didier Cambérabéro 50 pts in 4 games

Biggest wins overall

England: 1997 Ireland 6 England 46
difference: 40pts Lansdowne Road
France: 1998 France 51 Wales 0
difference: 51pts Wembley Stadium
Wales: 1910 Wales 49 France 14
difference: 35pts St Helens, Swansea
Scotland: 1912 Scotland 31 France 3
difference: 28 pts Inverleith, Edinburgh

and 1997 Scotland 38 Ireland 10
difference: 28pts Murrayfield
Ireland: 1913 Ireland 24 France 0
difference 24pts Cork

Biggest defeats overall

England: 1986 Scotland 33 England 6
difference: 27pts Murrayfield
France: 1910 Wales 49 France 14
difference: 35pts St Helens, Swansea
Wales: 1998 Wales 0 France 51
difference: 51pts Wembley Stadium
Scotland: 1998 Scotland 16 France 51
difference: 35pts Murrayfield
Ireland: 1997 Ireland 6 England 46
difference: 40pts Lansdowne Road

Highest overall win: 1998 France 51 Wales 0
difference: 51pts Wembley Stadium
Worst ever result: As above
Most points by a team in a match: 1998
England 60 Wales 26 Twickenham (difference 34)

Five Nations Table

	P	W	D	L	%Wins
Wales	376	198	23	155	53
England	368	182	38	148	50
France	279	133	17	129	48
Scotland	379	169	21	189	44
Ireland	378	161	23	194	43

Left to right: Will Carling has 40 Five Nations caps for England, while Paul Thorburn has scored 173 points for Wales, Alan Tait nine tries for Scotland, and Michael Kiernan 215 points for Ireland

MOST CAPPED PLAYERS COUNTRY BY COUNTRY

Five Nations games only

England
1. Rory Underwood . . . . . . .50 caps
2. Rob Andrews . . . . .40 caps
3. Will Carling . . . . .40 caps
4. Wade Dooley . . . . .33 caps
5. Brian Moore . . . . .33 caps

France
1. Philippe Sella . . . . .51 caps
2. Serge Blanco . . . . .42 caps
3. Jean-Pierre Rives . . . . .39 caps
4. Roland Bertranne . . . . .37 caps
5. Michel Crauste . . . . . . .35 caps

Ireland
1. Mike Gibson . . . . .56 caps
2. Willie John McBride . . . .53 caps
3. Fergus Slattery . . . . . . .47 caps
4. Phil Orr . . . . .46 caps
5. Tom Kiernan . . . . .44 caps

Scotland
1. Jim Renwick . . . . .42 caps
2. Scott Hastings . . . . . . .41 caps
3. Sandy Carmichael . . . . .41 caps
4. Andy Irvine . . . . .39 caps
5. Alastair McHarg . . . . . .37 caps
   Colin Deans . . . . .37 caps

Wales
1. JPR Williams . . . . .44 caps
2. Ieuan Evans . . . . .36 caps
3. Graham Price . . . . .35 caps
4. R M Owen . . . . .32 caps
5. Rob Jones . . . . .32 caps

FIVE NATIONS PLAYERS STATISTICS
ENGLAND
Top five try scorers in Five Nations
1. Rory Underwood . . . . . .20 tries
2. Kit Lowe . . . . .18 tries
3. John Birkett . . . . .10 tries
4. Jeremy Guscott . . . . . . .7 tries
5. Tony Underwood . . . . . . .7 tries

Overall highest points scorers in Five Nations
1. Rob Andrew 197pts
2. Paul Grayson 185pts
3. Dusty Hare 178pts
4. Jon Webb 157pts
5. Bob Hiller 122pts

SCOTLAND
Top five try scorers
1. Ian Smith . . . . .24 tries
2. Arthur Smith . . . . .10 tries
3. Alan Tait . . . . .9 tries
4. Tony Stanger . . . . .7 tries
5. Iwan Tukalo . . . . .6 tries

Overall highest points scorers
1. Gavin Hastings 333pts
2. Andy Irvine 201pts
3. Peter Dods 144pts
4. Craig Chalmers 136pts
5. Ian Smith 72pts

FRANCE
Top five try scorers
1. Serge Blanco . . . . .16 tries
2. Philippe Sella . . . . .15 tries
3. Philippe Saint-André . . .15 tries
4. Christian Darrouy . . . . .13 tries
5. Emile Ntamack . . . . . . .13 tries

Overall highest points scorers
1. Thierry Lacroix 151pts
2. Didier Cambérabéro 127pts
3. Serge Blanco 121pts
4. Jean-Pierre Romeu 103pts
5. Pierre Villepreux 89pts

WALES
Top five try scorers
1. Gareth Edwards . . . . . . .18 tries
2. Reggie Gibbs . . . . .17 tries
3. Gerald Davies . . . . .16 tries
4. Ken Jones . . . . .16 tries
5. Ieuan Evans . . . . .12 tries

Overall highest points scorers
1. Neil Jenkins 312pts
2. Paul Thorburn 173pts
3. Phil Bennett 149pts
4. Steve Fenwick 139pts
5. Jack Bancroft 89pts

IRELAND
Top five try scorers
1. George Stephenson . . . .14 tries
2. Brendan Mullin . . . . . . .11 tries
3. Allan Duggan . . . . .9 tries
4. Simon Geoghegan . . . . . .6 tries
5. Hugo MacNeill . . . . .5 tries

Overall highest points scorers
1. Michael Kiernan 215pts
2. Ollie Campbell 182pts
3. Eric Elwood 156pts
4. Tom Kiernan 124pts
5. Mike Gibson 92pts